THROW ME UNDER THE BUS...PLEASE

Jeffrey A. Miller

"Throw Me Under The Bus...Please," by Jeffrey A. Miller. ISBN 978-1-60264-302-4 (softcover) 978-1-60264-294-2 (ebook).

Published 2009 by Virtualbookworm.com Publishing Inc., P.O. Box 9949, College Station, TX 77842, US. ©2009, Jeffrey A. Miller. All rights reserved. No part of this publication may be reproduced, stored in a retrieval system, or transmitted in any form or by any means, electronic, mechanical, recording or otherwise, without the prior written permission of Jeffrey A. Miller.

Manufactured in the United States of America.

Dedicated to whoever developed the concept of the high speed limited access highway, without which this trip would have lasted even longer, and to the devoted individuals who clean the rest stops on the American interstate highway system and prevent them from resembling their far less immaculate counterparts south of the border.

PREFACE

Maybe I listen to too much National Public Radio. No, I am not an elbow-patch wearing, Pete Seeger worshiping, hotel towel reusing, liberal college philosophy professor. Nor do I sip Pinot Noir and nibble artisanal camembert while listening to Bach sonatas on a vinyl record. Simply put, I just loathe commercials. Furthermore, I am not musically inclined, so I generally avoid typical hip hop, classical, urban, country or even rock radio. Finally, I can only listen to so many commercial broadcast news traffic reports in an afternoon, detailing delays on the Long Island Expressway, oblivious to my unencumbered eight mile local commute on the side streets of northern New Jersey. I guess my self-described lack of musical inclination is a bit like referring to Vladimir Dracula as devoid of proper table manners. I took piano lessons for five years as a child and never graduated from the mandatory beginner's keyboard bible, *Thompson's Red Book*. Remember "The Wigwam Song" or "Song of the Volga Boatmen?" I do, as I played them, improperly, for half a decade. Ted, my first piano teacher, a young man with grand unanswered aspirations of becoming a concert pianist, eventually committed suicide. True story. However, I blame this tragedy on my brother, Neil; for as atrocious a musician as I proved to be, Neil, in opposition, made me appear as the reincarnation of Sergei Rachmaninov.

1

Regardless, I am often astonished by the myriad of TV and radio interviews with authors touting their personal memoirs. It seems like everyone whose past includes a notable feature or performance, from the Norwegian zoologist depicting the trials of potty training his pet orangutan to the blind grandmother who scaled Mount Everest confined to a wheelchair, without bottled oxygen of course, feels compelled to share his or her experience with the rest of mankind. The significance of these "accomplishments" is dubious at best. Nonetheless, there are millions of readers who seem enthralled by the first person depictions of such escapades.

I like to write. I figured maybe I could prepare my own memoir. Unfortunately, although I have led a successful, in most cases, enviable, life, I could find little so exceptional to be of interest to anyone other than myself. Not a very lucrative way to prepare a bestseller. My wife wouldn't buy a copy, even with my money. A dog might be loyal enough to purchase my memoir, but it would not be worth the payback of constant walks and separating table scraps. What a mundane life. I was never an alter boy at a Boston Catholic Church. I was not abused by my parents, unless one has ever had the misfortune to listen to my mother sit at the piano and recite the lyrics to such favorites as "Shoo Fly, Don't Bother Me," "Go Tell Aunt Rhody" or the entire score of "Fiddler on the Roof" in a key hereto only associated with a rusty chainsaw or wayward sanitation truck. I have a wonderful, devoted wife and two well behaved, healthy young sons. No philandering with lesbian rock stars, familial murder plots or, God forbid, rare childhood brain tumors in our history. I have never been kidnapped or circumnavigated the globe on a car tire. I am a physician, but alas, a radiologist. I save lives by sitting in a climate controlled office, sipping a cup of re-heated coffee, and detecting small, "precancerous" spots on chest x-rays and

CT scans. No chance of me removing a bullet fragment from a wounded president's left ventricle or parachuting into a Somalian war zone to save a captive village from ringworm infestation.

My memoir, therefore, is composed in juxtaposition to the above death defying situations and anomalous characters. I am just a guy who was thrust into a perfectly ordinary situation, but one that invokes a greater dread than any unguarded stockpile of weapons of mass destruction or box of a dozen trans-fat laden jelly donuts. I am the everyman, bearing my soul to report on the seemingly ordinary tribulations I faced on a trip to a foreign land (OK, it was only Mexico) with three generations of the five most important people in my life. This act appears, on the surface, to be mundane, which is the point. But for anyone who has ever attempted a similar feat of oppressive physical and emotional stress, such a journey is rife with situations, both pleasant and painful, to which we can all relate. Now, rather than having to experience such turmoil yourself, you will have the chance to live vicariously through another man's anxieties and snicker at his hapless misfortunes.

I. MIGHT AS WELL MEET THE FAMILY ALREADY

We haven't yet arranged for a cab to the airport for our imminent trip to Mexico, and I am already worried about the flight home to New Jersey. Unlike my sons, procrastination makes me anxious and Lord knows, I don't need any additional stress on this expedition. I have already taken the liberty to order a broccoli calzone, large salad, two slices of regular pizza, an eggplant Parmesan hero, and an order of peppers and eggs to be delivered at 7:30pm on the evening of our return. Of course, I realize that such forethought practically guarantees that our plane will be late, leaving the repast to freeze into a red, white and green facsimile of an off-day Henry Moore sculpture on the porch. However, between the raccoons, deer, ground hogs, osprey and occasional run-a-way dog that frequent our property, I am sure it will not go to waste. I will be left to ponder why God had enough foresight and commercial sensibility to create the menu of the typical pizzeria in the same colors as the Italian flag. Did he speak to the Italian tourism bureau first? I guess he doesn't need too. It's nice to be omniscient. It's even better to be the boss. Maybe if I make a habit of feeding our indigenous critters, they will stop frequenting our perennial gardens, flower beds, shrubbery and trash cans with the ferocity of a corps of

Throw Me Under The Bus...Please

marine recruits hitting the chow line after a thirty mile hike.

For anyone who needs to know these things, I wrote the first draft of this treatise with a free Commerce Bank ballpoint pen, in distinctive cobalt blue, on an undersized tablet of lined paper, also blue. The two shades of blue complement one another exquisitely, in the manner of a Picasso portrait, circa 1902. Yes, I can type. I was proudly recorded at 48 words per minute at the end of my 11th grade typing elective. It was, by a monumental degree, the most practical course in which I have ever enrolled. Indeed, we brought a laptop computer on the trip. Unfortunately, during the entire week, I was unable to wrestle it from my sons, whose infatuation with computer games is only matched by their appetite for rib eye steak, medium rare. Unfortunately, as I scribbled the majority of my notes in the cramped seat of a moving bus, they are nearly illegible, even to my own trained eyes. I will have to "wing it," and pray that I have a more precise recall of our journey than President Reagan had concerning a certain international armament deal. I share neither his political clout nor his charisma, although I surmise that, near the end, his handwriting probably bore a general resemblance to my current vibration-aided scrawl.

As related in the Preface section, by profession, I am a radiologist. Although officially a well trained physician, in practice, I and my colleagues are just over-educated, less eloquent photography critics. I spend my days (and many evenings) staring at a pair of over-sized, high resolution computer screens, studying images of fractured bones, pneumonias and tumors, and dictating my opinions concerning those pictures back to the machine. Not exactly your clichéd, yet non-existent, country doctor traversing the county with his omnipresent black bag dispensing comfort and medications to the ill. I don't even own, nor remember how to use, a stethoscope. If only some 14 year-old graduate student at MIT were able to program the computer to do an acceptable job interpreting those images without a radiologist's input, my job would be much less arduous. I would also be unemployed, making it difficult to supply the boys with their requisite rations of red meat, chocolate chip cookies and shoes of a never ending, upward spiral of sizes. On the positive side, writing the first draft of this memoir in long hand on a paper pad, which I guess would be described as "analog" communication in today's parlance, detached me from my digitally controlled professional responsibilities. I can envision myself crouching in the depths of a prehistoric French cave, painting depictions of woolly mammoths (or is it "mammi?") on the dank, insect laden, unlit stone walls. Just me and my imagination, fighting the elements, crushed-berry paint smeared on my hands and stalactites dripping fetid water on my forehead. Without a doubt, there would also be a drooling saber-toothed tiger parked, famished, at the entranceway. OK, maybe being a 21st century radiologist, sitting in a sterile air-conditioned office, talking to a whirring device that reiterates everything I say as if I were David Koresh leading the Branch Davidians, may not be so bad after all.

With that said, I have a message for any descendants who might find this note pad buried in some isolated basement corner while scouring our house for booty after we have departed. Of course, I am referring to migrating to Miami, not the afterlife, so kids please keep your paws off any misplaced jewelry or old coins. This tale has been written in the proper form of our much bastardized basic language, English. This obscure language is guided by centuries-old rules of propriety which already have been largely displaced by the need for urgency, aided by the myriad of new communication devices available to the market. I hope, however, that in the near future, technology will return what it has currently purloined. In

Throw Me Under The Bus...Please

this regard, I assume that in the future there will be no more text messaging or blogs. My as yet unborn grandchildren will again be rewarded with the ability to speak and write in the most perfect Elizabethan prose. Only this gift will be enabled by some sort of microchip embedded in their brains at birth, bouncing microwaves off a massive computer server on Venus. These electronic signals will transcribe the most subtle subconscious thoughts into beautifully formulated sentences and paragraphs in a manner that would make Faulkner weep with envy. As for the current generation of youth, please don't ask me, "Who is Faulkner?"

I guess this is a good spot to quickly depict the cast of characters, here-before known as my immediate family. In order of age, my Mom, Elaine, has 12 days on my father. Although a septuagenarian, she is still a practicing attorney, specializing in what she calls, "family oriented law," particularly as it relates to child custody issues. She is one of the first of the breed of "supermoms" (who have subsequently matured into "super grandmoms"), working full time in family court and her private office, in addition to laboring through all the cooking, housework, gardening, shopping and laundry for her household. This household, in a reversal of the classic "empty nest," has re-expanded recently to include my 40-something-year-old brother, my older sister and her two kids, as well as my father. Mom possesses an interesting combination of being both an exceedingly private individual and an outward social butterfly, never one to miss a concert, museum opening, Bar Mitzvah, first communion, or Tet celebration. Unfortunately, sometimes in her relentless pursuit of life's abundant menu of entrees, she foregoes some of the more mundane ingredients of the stew. There is little physical strength or mental storage remaining for such banal concepts as her oldest son's address, her grandchildren's birthdays, or on occasion, brushing her hair.

My father is a pulmonologist. Medicine still fascinates him after almost half a century of practice. He is the consummate intellectual, a person in love with knowledge. The man is able to find the cerebral facet of virtually any activity, be it a conference on ancient Babylonian glassware or a cartoon video about mixed martial arts. Unfortunately, he manages largely to avoid the very powerful influences of popular culture, considered not worthy of occupying valuable neural synapses. Sometimes it is difficult to talk to a man who can rattle off the birth date of Ulysses (be it the Greek poet or the late president and civil war commander) but thinks Britney Spears is a type of medieval French weapon of war. He has always been physically active, but lately has been hampered by an exquisitely painful foot injury and worsening spinal stenosis. I shouldn't even get into the urethral stricture, the result of a flawed prostate surgery performed by one of his old cronies. Needless to report, with just a touch of irony, said urologist died only a few months after the procedure as a complication of Parkinson Disease. Shaking hands and delicate surgery on ones most valued anatomic feature are not typically the ingredients of a successful procedure. Dad vowed that these physical maladies would never affect his ability to partake in every aspect of our Mexican tour. We shall see. One last note to stir the pot: Both my parents are very generous with their time and money, but their charity is often dispensed in the form of a contract with the Devil. The recipient often must relinquish any concept of control in return for the acquisition of these lavish gifts. I sold my soul for a free family trip south of the border. Good intentions by Mom and Dad, probably. A fiasco in the making, definitely.

Throw Me Under The Bus...Please

Sharon, my wife, is a microbiologist by trade who gave up her profession when our first child was born. She has been unquestionably more valuable in her current role as family manager. We need her services more than the bacteria do. Sharon does not possess my mother's obsession for charging in the manner of a deranged mongoose at every aspect of her life, but is infinitely more organized than any of us. She has become the rock to which I anchor my emotions and travails. She is slavishly devoted to the welfare of our kids, her widowed mother and, although I hate to admit it, her husband. In return, aside from maintaining a source of income, which is the easy part, I must occasionally bear the aftermath of her own emotional upheavals. The woman to whom everyone turns in time of crises must occasionally unload those demons somewhere, and thus steps in, often unwittingly, her husband. As we have seen, the term, "meek," does not apply to my family. I can attest that it is wholly within character for my most beloved football and boxing "buddy" to be my wife. Pity the poor soul who harkens the "wrath of Sharon" by interrupting her enjoyment of the Sunday NFL pre-game shows. She can also indulge in the ancient sporting ritual of voluminous foaming adult beverage ingestion without showing the least sign of ethanol-related dysfunction. I must admit, however, that although she is genuinely engrossed in the reports of the on-field battle, Sharon displays a greater interest than the average male viewer in the attire and coiffures of the recently retired hunks who serve as sports announcers.

 A week with her in-laws on a tour through a foreign land leaves much room for toes to be squashed, purposely or not, and space to be invaded. Fortunately, Sharon, with a little charm and a lot of free will, has the ability not only to survive a stint in such a mine field of emotions, but to protect her husband and genuinely enjoy herself in the

Jeffrey A. Miller

process. With that rare gift for defusing impending salvos in mind, the Cambodian government would do well to hire her to clear their jungles of residual Vietnam War era unexploded munitions. I, on the other hand, lack my wife's tact and rosy demeanor. Sharon would prance through the remaining South Asian booby traps, angry at her tormentors but physically and mentally unscathed. I, on the other hand, would resemble Wile E. Coyote after opening a "Christmas present" from the Roadrunner; black soot covering my face, a full body cast entrapping my torso and yellow whistling stars encircling my head.

It is amazing how the male animal can function in all realms of life prior to marriage; obtaining nutrients, laundering clothes, using the telephone and even occasionally (very occasionally) scrubbing the bathroom. After wedlock, the minuscule portion of the masculine brain not directly involved with earning money, screaming at a shortstop's errant throw to first base, or the improper use of power tools, almost immediately involutes and necroses. A few residual neurons are retained for the sole purpose of ordering a hamburger and beer in an emergency when the wife is not home to cook or choose dinner. Long ago, Sharon realized this sorry paroxysm of male evolution and took pity upon me. She has taken it upon herself to personally compensate for, or even replace, my lost capabilities. Not only did Sharon make all the flight reservations for the trip, research each hotel, provide all the material goods necessary to keep the kids happy and even remember to discontinue our newspaper subscriptions, but she took complete charge of packing each of our suitcases. She developed a fool-proof system of keeping her legions clean and respectable. Every day, each male member of the family was provided with a pair of shorts and a clean t-shirt for the daily trek and a second fresh, collared shirt for dinner. The previous evening's shorts would be worn on the next day's

Throw Me Under The Bus...Please

journey, matched with another fresh t-shirt. A complete pair of laundered shorts and appropriate collared shirt was again set aside for dinner. Each day's attire was packaged together in the suitcase, making the entire process of maintaining some semblance of personal appearance a virtually brainless endeavor. All I had to remember was to pack enough underwear for the week as well as a bathing suit and a couple pairs of sneakers. I am happy to report that I managed to bring the sneakers and bathing suit, two in fact. Somehow, though, I managed to miscalculate the number of days in a week and ended up with at least six superfluous pairs of men's briefs. It is best to err on the safe side when apportioning such a necessity. Sorry to those ladies to whom this matters, but there are no boxers in my ensemble.

As for me, I hope you noticed that in this chronological list of personalities, Sharon's name is positioned before mine. For the nine months per year that she is officially registered as my senior, this unyielding mathematic discrepancy provides her with no small degree of angst. No one embraces my birthday more than she, as it brings an equivalence of our stated ages, if only temporarily.

The overlap in my father's and my career, although unintentional, was not wholly coincidental, either. It has, for the most part, bolstered our relationship, both on the professional and personal level. In contrast to Dad's unremitting enthusiasm for science and medicine, my relative nonchalance towards his Holy Grail has also served as a source of quiet conflict. My mind definitely works on a mathematical, research-grounded algorithm and I find health care both an interesting and, at least on the surface, altruistic means of earning a living. I take pride in my knowledge base and diagnostic skills. Unlike Dad, however, I would rather watch a football game, take a few laps in the pool or watch an old B-movie on cable

TV than search for another pneumonia on a chest x-ray or discuss the MRI characteristics of benign adrenal gland tumors with my colleagues.

In deference to my maternal genes, I too have little tolerance for remaining sedentary. I am most comfortable multi-tasking, but not quite to Mom's level of distraction. I tend to be more focused on the particular project at hand. I find that an approximately eighty percent to twenty percent split in my attention between primary pursuit and extraneous matters provides the most efficient utilization of mind and body. As for my personality, it can best be summarized as cynical to the point of being sardonic. If I can allow myself a few clichés, there are no rose colored glasses in my bureau and all the cups in our cabinets seem hopelessly half, or more typically three-quarters, empty. However, I do not consider myself a depressive personality. I maintain a relatively flat persona regardless of the situation, with few peaks and valleys. Consider me Kansas in a continent of Colorado's.

If you are wondering about my personal appearance, Sharon thinks I am too skinny. But you know what they say about never being too rich or too thin. Since we are not wealthy, that leaves only a low body fat index to elicit the envy of my neighbors. No violins, please, we live quite comfortably, with all the familial love and material goods anyone could ever want. Unfortunately, we are genetically programmed with a capitalistic disposition. More is always better. Unless, of course, one is describing his or her adipose tissue.

If it doesn't become obvious during the narration of this tale, I tend to be rather self-denigrating. Although some amateur psychiatrists may consider it a sign of self-confidence, in my case it is probably the opposite. Belittling my own piddling merits transforms me into an instant underdog, whose every minor victory will be applauded in the manner of a reserve quarterback's ninety yard touchdown pass; understudy prima donnas glass-breaking aria; or a toddler's first full night with a dry diaper. Furthermore, I have found that nothing, not getting lost in ones own neighborhood, giving a lecture with ones fly unzipped, or breaking an ankle attempting to imitate Fred Astaire at a cousin's wedding, can deflate one's ego like the words and actions of one's own pre-teen sons. Regardless of what I wear, how I speak or who I admire, it is considered outdated. I could discover a cure for cancer and devise a means of universally distributing it via low energy microwaves and my kids would berate me for being an old fashioned nerd. "No one bothers with microwaves anymore, Dad," would be a typical reaction. "Why should I care that you made the front page of the New York Times? None of my friends read newspapers," would be another retort. Only when I remind them of the monetary rewards of such an endeavor and the possibility of a "trickle down" to my offspring would I get a positive response. Their acceptance would last just long enough to procure a few dollars and run off, without their embarrassing old man, to the video game store.

One last note that may help clarify the ensuing tale. Although I enjoy experiencing new lands and cultures, I loathe the act of traveling itself. Planes and buses are my personal gulag. Therefore, to put it metaphorically, the foundation of the Mexican tour was poured with a large crack before the upper floors were assembled. In my opinion, even a week in the Garden of Eden, prior to the infamous apple incident, would prove to be an odious journey were it to require a bus. I was never a fan of the old TV series, "Star Trek," but the words, "Beam me up, Sharon," would have gone a long way towards improving this fiasco loosely disguised as a vacation.

Jared, my eldest child, is 12. He has managed the art of accumulating more facts and insight concerning history, science, culture and current events than the entire editorial staff of the New York Times. Amazingly, he has managed to morph into a living encyclopedia without ever applying any of his vast database of knowledge to school. Jared has always been my unfaltering pal, constantly by my side, and would do anything within his powers to avoid hurting my feelings. My greatest qualm with my elder son is his infatuation with video and computer games. I realize that I am from another era, but his mindless, gripping obsession with the machinations of the artificial characters on a fluorescent monitor is beyond my comprehension. Early in our marriage, I thought that having kids would provide me an excuse to limber up the ol' pitching arm or pump up the tires on my bike. Dad and his boys—a three-man playground sports contingent. Sadly, my most important role in Jared's play appears to be re-setting the wifi connection when it goes on the fritz. Nonetheless, he possesses one of the most sophisticated senses of humor I have ever witnessed in a child and is the source of endless conversations on subjects ranging from the stock market to Voltaire. Jared's laid back demeanor and easy going but helpful nature are a source of instant popularity with all he meets, whether he cares for their outreach or not. Incidentally, Jared's physique makes mine look hefty, only he manages to maintain it on an 8000 calorie/day diet.

Raphael is approaching his tenth birthday. Where Jared is reserved, Raphi is in-your-face direct, often with an underpinning of mockery for good measure. Nothing gets by his gaze and he lets you know it. Raphi has the more artistic bent of the two, excelling in the structural arts, writing and also in possession of a deep appreciation for music. He is also the more socially conventional of the two. Jared, although having several friends whom he will likely retain for life, enjoys his personal space. Raphi prefers company at all times, at least after about 1:00pm when he finally finds the energy to change out of his pajamas, and becomes much more attuned to the social mores of the day. He is also a very competitive young man, much more driven towards perfection in his work and his play than his older brother. Both children never fail to amaze me with their level of maturity, however. I must admit, as their parent, their behavior, especially in public situations, is impeccable. They have vast interests and throughout their lives, even as toddlers, could be appropriately entertained in virtually any situation. Sharon and I have always spoken to them at a plane slightly above their level of complete comprehension and have taken them to a panoply of museums, restaurants and destinations meant for more mature audiences. In return, they have not only adapted to but have excelled in these environments. All the while, they maintain an uncanny respect for both their peers, their elders and even complete strangers. I wish, at 45, I could act as mature in the presence of my parents as they display in the presence of theirs. But then, this tale wouldn't be very interesting, would it?

While I'm at it, I might as well mention the rest of my immediate family, although they have no direct significance to this Mexican adventure. I am providing this brief synopsis, in part for completeness, to aid in deciphering the foibles of my background. More significantly, if I don't add their names, they will never forgive the oversight. Holiday dinners would become hostile skirmishes, with yours truly as the sole target of the sniper's bullets and roadside bombs, rather than the simple festivals of intended spiritual enlightenment, linguistic drivel and culinary excess they are now. Dina, my elder sister is a physician who also lives on Long Island with her two kids, Morgan and Malcah, about a mile from my parents. Neil, my younger brother, who has always been more than a brother, but my closest confident and sounding board, lives in the third leg of the geographic triangle, about a mile from Dina and my parents. He blissfully has gone through life with no significant other and no children of his own. He has become a surrogate father not only to the entire high school in which he teaches, but to our nephew and niece down the road. My younger sister, Michele, lives in Westchester County, north of New York City. Although quite an intellectual, with a PhD in archeology from Stanford University, she is now maintaining an enviable lifestyle with her husband, Matt, a successful lawyer in the finance industry, and their two adorable young boys, Josh and Jake. Josh will forever be my special link to the future, as we share the same birthday as well as similar good looks. I assume he will maintain his handsome appearance further into the future than I. He is already much more personable than I am, as well. Lastly, I will tip my hat to my Uncle Gerry and Aunt Roz, who, completely by coincidence, live only a few miles north of us. They can be considered the unintentional, nascent enablers of this trip, as it is they who planted the seeds of my cherished marriage to Sharon via a blind date fifteen years in the past.

For those readers still interested in our journey south of the border, I am sorry for this last, rather gratuitous paragraph. I probably would have created more interest had I included a page involving lust, sweat and a vivid sexual encounter, but Sharon read the draft and only giggled. She reminded me that as a memoir, the actions in this tale are supposed to be factual. Another blow to my ego better off deleted. Maybe I should add a few lines more relevant to my life instead, delineating my role in the slightly less passionate tasks of taking out the garbage, unclogging toilets, or rendering final rights for deceased hermit crabs and goldfish.

II. CAN YOU GET IN THE CAB ALREADY

Enough musing about my family, the mundane aspects of my career and my haughty protection of traditional written language. I am sure you would rather hear about the tribulations of our trip than the general eccentricities of the Miller clan. We ordered our taxi pick up for only an hour and 45 minutes before the scheduled airline departure. Two hours leeway seemed sheepishly long, the realm of airport neophytes, but an hour and a half seemed destined to invoke an unnecessary level of anxiety. Did I mention that I am a little fixated with time? I wear two watches. On my right wrist hangs a waterproof plastic digital model costing $8.00 on the street on front of Madison Square Garden. I gaze at it constantly. My left wrist supports a self-winding, conventional faced Hublot time piece, costing many times as much. It is very attractive, but I rarely glance at it. It is for the envious eyes of others, sort of a miniature Porsche or yacht, intended primarily to boost my own sensation of self worth.

Our ride to Newark Liberty International Airport was a mere 22 minutes, aided by a rare lack of traffic. We had our usual, Livingston Taxi Company, overly loquacious, "know-it-all" driver. Somehow, at least according to his monologue, he had dined at every upscale restaurant in Essex County and had vacationed at every tropical destination in either hemisphere. A rather impressive social calendar on a cab driver's salary, I must admit. Maybe he married a wealthy heiress and only drives his aged Chevy Impala taxi as a break from the sticky leather upholstery and overstated elegance of his Bentley. However, his cheerfulness and eagerness to relieve us of the burden of our baggage was much appreciated. If nothing else, he laughed vociferously at even my lamest jokes as the rest of the vehicle fell silent with the embarrassed resignation of familiarity. Of course, his strategy worked. Sustaining my ego earned him a hefty tip at the termination of the ride. Now it made sense. He lived lavishly on the fortune from gratuities he wrangled from striving comedian schnooks like me.

The trip to the airport allowed me a few minutes to muse upon the origins of our forthcoming journey south. My parents have long complained that because of the relative distance between our abodes as well as our conflicting employment and social schedules, they have little chance to spend good, sorry for the cliché, "quality time," with their grandsons. Although actually only 47 miles, the necessity to cross a combination of two bridges and/or tunnels and traverse vast portions of New York City make the actual mileage inconsequential. A trip to Grandma's house could take up to three hours, even without the threat of being eaten by Red Riding Hood's nemesis, the Big Bad Wolf. I would much prefer to face the fangs of said famished, overgrown canine than the traffic caused by a jack-knifed tractor trailer on the Cross Bronx Expressway. My parents are absolutely correct however, and I often lament the lack of informality and spontaneity in our relationship. The kids have so much to learn from their elders and, likewise, the boys' excellent behavior and inquisitive nature are a source of endless pride to their Mom and Dad.

Throw Me Under The Bus...Please

Therefore, they offered to pay for airfare and lodging if we joined them on vacation to a warm destination during the boys' Presidents Day school break. On paper, it sounded like a wonderful deal for a miser like myself. Pleasant weather, a change of scenery and three generations joined in family togetherness with little monetary risk to yours truly. However, my parents' notion of a vacation shares little with Sharon's or my own. They seek education and novelty rather than relaxation. Fortunately, although tropical, Guantanamo Bay was off-limits to tourists; Paris Island required a two year commitment in fashion deprived olive drab baggy pants; and Haiti's major hotels had long been disassembled for firewood by the desperate populace. The boys, on the other hand, are not so picky. They are happy as long as there is enough to eat, a ready source of electricity for their various media devices and the rarified comfort of universally available air conditioning. Sharon and I lobbied for a simple week at a beach resort, preferably in the proximity of a plethora of non-aquatic activities as insurance against the omnipresent rain that seems to shadow our vacations in the manner of a hungry puppy pawing a third grader's lunch box. I also desired an easily accessible airport, to ease the strain of travel, as well as a stay in a standard modern resort hotel. I despise the currently de rigor "boutique" hotels that resemble a cleaner, funky version of a University of Arizona fraternity house. In the opposite vein, I will not sleep in a tent or bathe under a waterfall, either. Such destinations as the Bahamas, Cancun, Puerto Rico or even that modern Catskills of the South, Miami, would have been welcome. Although I have visited the "hurricane city" at least two dozen times in my life, it caters to a compendium of common needs necessary to ensure a pleasant, painless week of relaxation. There are non-stop flights departing every 20 seconds; endless hotel choices; clean, free beaches frequented by attractive European model-types; a myriad of dining choices ranging from edible sushi to fresh local fish and the only semi-authentic bagels outside of New York; and plenty of both cultural and populist forms of entertainment away from the beach and pool.

Unfortunately, my parents, who are avid travelers, tend to seek slightly less banal destinations. I would have compromised with a week in Antigua, the Cayman Islands or other such tucked-away faux paradise, but those and similar choices were nixed as being too boring. At least Mom and Dad had no desire to embark on a cruise. Ocean liners, to me, are akin to whitewashed floating prisons, only with better food, safer showers and an anatomically correct female roommate. Furthermore, the medical consultant in me could do without spending my vacation in what is essentially an 800 foot, quarter billion dollar petri dish, inoculated with a combination of 3000 blowing noses and wiping rear ends, 14 metric tons of whitefish salad, and a beating tropical sun. As an added attraction, the inhabitants and their effluent freely share a common closed sewage system.

However, I was not prepared for Mom's eventual decision. Since we could not agree upon a suitable destination, there would be none. Instead, they had reserved six spots on a guided group tour of the wonders of pre-Columbian Mexican architecture. It sounded like one of those college courses one takes just to fulfill the credit requirements in the humanities, outside one's major. We would spend our Presidents Week vacation on a bus in southeastern Mexico. In between jaunts down the highway, we would have the opportunity to climb the stairs lining the walls of innumerable stone buildings, listen to lectures on Mexican history and be herded around in precisely choreographed precision between gift shops, rest stops and early morning hotel wake-up calls. All of this would be shared with forty of the

Throw Me Under The Bus...Please

aforementioned Public Radio listening, Volvo driving, Birkenstock wearing colleagues alluded to above. To my dismay, Sharon and the boys, desperate for a spot of warm weather and change of scenery and fearful of further inertia if we were to turn down the offer, agreed to the trip. I had no choice but to join the crowd, lest I remain at home alone for the week, left to read my x-rays and dine on whatever leftovers I could chisel from the back of the freezer, in solitude. To make matters worse, without Jared's electronic intuition, I would remain befuddled by the remote control, if I could find it, as I attempt to watch an "on demand" movie on the big screen TV.

Once inside the terminal, the security lines moved with respectable efficiency, an observation we have surprisingly made on many previous passages through Newark Liberty Airport. A little New Jersey machismo on the part of the security inspectors, combined with bored resignation by us early morning travelers led to a rapid dissemination of the snaking cues. This may seem as a bit of a conundrum at the airport widely reported persistently to lead the nation in flight delays. I try to maintain a positive stance. It provides us Garden State travelers with more time to fight for one of the few remaining seats at our assigned gate as we settle in for the long bleak wait for the distant mechanical bird. A rare treat, however, was provided by the virtually on-time departure of our Continental 737–800. I have long given up the notion of being treated as anything other than a fattened veal in a Texas feed-lot while in flight, so a timely departure hopefully translating into an equally perfunctory arrival must suffice as an answer to my prayers. I try to ignore the fact that the young bovine, in the name of prime fat marbling, is ensured of a satisfying, nutritious repast as he awaits his fate. I am not sure what well intentioned consultant informed the Continental Airlines management that humans prefer to eat mucinous turkey pastrami on a still-frozen roll at every meal, regardless of time of day, but I am sure he was rewarded with a substantial bonus. The next time I enjoy a grilled veal chop, well marbled with fat, of course, I will be satisfied with revenge at that young calf's sated belly.

The flight to Mexico City was uneventful. The movie du jour was "The Jane Austen Book Club," a film I would never have agreed to watch had I not been strapped to a rigid seat 37,000 feet above terra firma, the epitome of the captive audience. Sharon, however, is a diligent fan of Ms. Austen, and was thrilled with her unexpected good fortune. If nothing else, I figured, the movie may give me some insight into the female infatuation with Austen's work and would provide a basis for a future literary discussion with my spouse. The movie, although essentially a soap opera, a form of entertainment neither of us ever followed, was actually rather entertaining. As had a number of the male subjects of the movie, I volunteered to read an Austen novel of Sharon's choice. The male characters were all real "guys," diving into their quest with typical macho skepticism. Each, of course, ended the movie appreciating Austen and her reparative powers on his particular social or romantic circumstance. I volunteered my services too quickly. Sharon, as if on cue, whipped out a copy of *Pride and Prejudice*, offering it as the perfect cure for the hours of highway monotony awaiting us in Mexico. I soon would learn why such movies are considered fiction. Even on a five hour bus ride, I would discover that counting the little hooks and loops on the Velcro head rest on the adjacent seat to be more engrossing than Ms. Austen's prose. A pity, actually, as Austen wrote beautifully from a stylistic perspective. I just could not become emotional over Darcy's prospects for marriage or which daughter would get the first dance at the umpteenth costume ball. Why couldn't Austen utilize her gift with English prose to compose a novel of with a more significant, or at least more exciting, plot line? Maybe the characters could all pack off on a frigate for a good old fashioned naval battle or at least a few weeks of island hopping and storm surviving in Tahiti.

III. FINALLY, WE ARRIVE

After a long flight, it was soothing to learn that the entrepreneurs at the Mexico City Airport were well schooled at the universal power of the American dollar and, I am sure, the Japanese yen, Chinese Yuan, European Union Euro and Russian Ruble as well. One's facial features are scrutinized more thoroughly and bags examined more diligently upon entering the Metropolitan Museum of Art than they are at Mexican customs. All the better to enhance the flow of tourist dollars into the local economy. The notion of a crazed but highly cultured suicide bomber sneaking into the impressionist gallery and reaping international havoc by blowing apart Monet's "Water Lilies" always struck me as a little perverse, anyway. I could have hidden an entire village's population of undocumented migrant workers returning home from cauliflower picking season in my carry-on without invoking a raised eyebrow from the customs officers. But then again, on their behalf, there are not many Americans trying to sneak into Mexico to mow lawns or fill wealthy Mexicans' water glasses at upscale restaurants. Best of all, the customs station was adjacent the first in a long parade of duty free shops so proud of their extensive selections of native tequila and mescal that they provided free tastings of their most prized spirits to anyone willing to ask. We asked more than once, the better to sample a wider array of beverages and to ease our arrival at the hotel and the requisite touring company welcome lecture. Needless to say, I remember little about the cab ride to the hotel, other than the obvious lack of public funds as compared to a typical American city. For example, the basic Mexico City public bus looked like it had been bartered from a Korean War army surplus lot, packed with a battalion's worth of human commuters and maybe a few chickens and dogs. The streets were relatively clean and although frenetic, both human and auto traffic appeared to roll in a relatively orderly manner.

Dinner was the first of many Mexican hotel buffet affairs, unfortunately included with the price of the tour. The food and ambiance bore a distinct resemblance to my New England college dining hall and the menu about as authentically Mexican. I never realized that iceberg lettuce with Italian dressing and potatoes au gratin were staples of our southern neighbor's cuisine. Not a refried bean, tortilla or even sprig of cilantro in sight. The selection of the beers (available, of course, for an additional fee) was actually Mexican in origin, but comprised of the same Corona, Dos Equis and Modelo Negro universally available, more thoroughly chilled, in the States. The native brews were just as tasteless and bland in their homeland as in New Jersey. Don't even ask about the Margaritas. Yes, I should not have been surprised. I know they are not an authentic Mexican concoction. Rather, according to legend, they were conjured up at a Palm Springs resort to replace the sting of the more traditional shot of tequila with slice of lime from the delicate tongues of the nouveau riche post World War II gringos who frequented the region. Somehow, substituting lime Kool-Aide and grain alcohol for tequila, Cointreau and fresh lime juice is sacrilegious, even towards a cocktail first created in the name of deception. The post dinner welcoming lecture, basically outlining the do's and don'ts of the tour, was, in the manner of our dinner, less than memorable. Sharon and I felt as if we

Jeffrey A. Miller

had interrupted a meeting at the local VFW, with grey hair, liver spots and rumpled beige shorts defining the style of the evening (and every day thereafter, as well). So much for long hikes through the jungle. The only strenuous activity for this crowd would come at the frequent rest stops when these geezers would try to pee against the resistance of their enlarged geriatric prostate glands or attempt a "number two" without the aid of their usual prune juice and Metamucil.

IV. SATURDAY, DAY TWO: MEXICO CITY AND TEOTIHUACAN

An early morning run around the perimeter of the park adjacent our hotel preceded our trip to Teotihuacan. We were warned by many sources concerning the dangers one would confront in the wee hours on the streets of the city. However, there appeared to be no time of the day or night desolate enough to entice the criminal elements. The early morning streets were not exactly teaming but were quite lively, even before 5am. Police, in cars and on foot, were stationed at every corner. I never felt unsafe or apprehensive and was never harassed, either by a suspicious civilian or by one of the notoriously corrupt officers. Best of all, I felt no deleterious respiratory effects from the famed pollution and high altitude of Mexico City. My lungs must have developed a tolerance in the automobile-perfumed atmosphere of suburban New Jersey.

Breakfast was at seven o'clock, which, as is my life-long habit, I deferred. By report, from the kids who never met a buffet they wouldn't attempt, and Sharon who prefers an unaccompanied morning cup of tea but has accepted the unenviable roll of vacation breakfast escort to the boys, the morning buffet was more authentic and contained a greater abundance of local produce than dinner. We had to be on the bus by eight. It was quite apparent from the onset that Pepe, our guide for the week, was as much a faithful slave of Father Time as I. He managed the clock like a veteran football coach approaching the two minute warning, even though, unlike myself, he wore only a single time piece. I never asked, but he must have had a military background. Eight o'clock meant precisely that. So much for the Hollywood clichés about Mexicans and their "mañana" attitude. I heralded this punctuality. Dad, on the other hand, has always attempted to manipulate Einstein's famed work on relativity by bending time around his own personal agenda. This generally runs at least thirty minutes behind everyone else's schedule. The ingredients were in line for a long week of temporal clashes.

The ride to Teotihuacan, although about ninety minutes long, would, in comparison to the transcontinental voyages awaiting us later in the week, seem in retrospect to be a brief jaunt down the road. The bus was modern and air conditioned, with double rows of reclining seats down its length. We were informed that we would be assigned positions on a strict rotating basis. The inhabitants of the front seats would slide to the far back and each preceding pair would move up one row upon each repeat boarding. Pepe decreed this arrangement as a point of law, but with no indication of the punishment awaiting those who failed to follow this precise choreography. However, in contrast to the egalitarian plan for the vehicle as a whole, the arrangement of personnel within our family's block of three pairs of seats had the potential for becoming a matter of extreme duress. Fortunately Mom and Dad were the last ones on the bus, leaving them to sit side by side in the only remaining row. I, as per usual in such situations, sat with Jared and Sharon with Raphi. Pepe kept us entertained on the trip with a constant stream of trivia about the surroundings, further delaying my literary rendezvous with Jane Austen.

Throw Me Under The Bus...Please

Upon arrival, we were met by a phalanx of indigenous entrepreneurs fighting to sell us their wares. It soon became quite apparent that they all sold basically the same item at similar prices. Even after the most energetic session of bargaining, the final price was always identical between seemingly competing merchants. Obviously, there was more than a bit of collusion going on. For all we knew, they were all in the same family or were all employed by some conglomerate working behind the scenes. Nonetheless, I briefly felt a tinge of guilt at quibbling over a single peso with person whose weekly earnings were probably less than the cost of a beer at our lunch buffet. In short order, however, I was able to convince myself that my purchase, regardless of my apparent pecuniary skills, would always extend a welcome profit to the vendor. They were quite savvy, I agreed, and were not about to take a monetary loss on any deal. Thus, both of us benefited as many of the statuettes, particularly those derived of lustrous black onyx, were quite attractive and still a veritable steal by US standards. Shaving off a few pesos at the bargaining table only added to the exotic nature of the crafts and was a boost to my innate competitive pride. The indigenous salesperson, I am sure, felt the same triumph at having unloaded a little onyx turtle on yet another boorish, egomaniacal tourist for the comparatively outrageous equivalent price of ten dollars when it only cost him a few pesos to manufacture. This model which takes advantage of the innate monetary indiscrepancies between a luxury laden economy with its inherent high cost of living and labor and a relatively indigent second or third world society has been the basis of foreign trade since prebiblical times. All parties prosper, even the chiropractors and orthopedists destined to treat the herniated discs and dislocated shoulders acquired as the uncontrollable tourists lug satchels of booty up and down pyramid stairs, into and out of buses and hotel elevators and eventually, through miles of airport terminals. A 1200 dollar medical bill is a small price to pay for the psychological reward of saving 45 cents on a wooden salad fork, hand embossed with a multicolored image of a jaguar.

The two most notable structures at Teotihuacan are two enormous pyramids named for the Moon and the Sun. They and the surrounding structures were erected by a civilization with no definable name and no known origin that disappeared without a trace, over a millennium ago. They could not have been assimilated into Aztec culture, as they preceded their future more famous neighbors by hundreds of years. Even more compelling, images the temples of the Sun and Moon have since become national icons, symbols of Mexico's rich native cultural heritage. I find it a bit perverse to rest a nation's identity upon the shoulders of a people who, save for the supposed evidence imparted by a pair of behemoth stone structures, may never have actually existed. Maybe they were constructed in secret by the Mexican Tourist Bureau to bolster sightseeing profits. Then again, perhaps they are the remnants of a set for a Cecil B. Demil epic on native Central American history, starring the late Charlton Heston as a renegade Aztec slave, which ran out of funding prior to completion.

In a similar vein, Aquino, our local tour guide du jour, pointed out that the original portions of a structure could easily be distinguished from reproduction work as the new walls were purposely constructed with small black stones embedded within the mortar. By my non-scientific count, approximately 90% of the buildings I surveyed contained only mortar lined by the aforementioned telltale stones. Very little of the site was original. More fodder for my theory that the ancient city of Teotihuacán was all a scam, built by legions of 20th Century entrepreneurs seeking a site to attract gullible

Throw Me Under The Bus...Please

American tourists vying to empty their wallets for engraved onyx letter openers, brass sun god pendants and 100% cotton t-shirts emblazoned with wash and wear Incan idols, native to Peru. Why else do we have such detailed records of the Mayan, Toltec and Aztec civilizations, but don't even know the name of the supposed society that erected the architectural marvels of Teotihuacan? I should be less cynical. It is best to take the view that regardless of who built them, whether by hemp rope and stone axes or pneumatic jackhammer and diesel crane, the pyramids are pretty spectacular and afford a great view of central Mexico from the top.

After an hour of being accosted by native merchants, whose rudimentary knowledge of English was still more comprehensible than our guide, Aquino's, we were afforded the pleasure of ascending to the top of the Pyramid of the Sun. Before us lay somewhere between 230 and 320 of the steepest yet narrowest stairs ever devised for two legged travel. Jared volunteered to count the steps as we climbed, but lost precise count at twelve. The rest is an estimate. Either the original inhabitants had the longest legs and shortest feet of any humanoids yet discovered or there was a secret elevator hidden somewhere in the middle of the structure. After spending the previous day on a plane and the morning on the dreaded bus, I actually looked forward to the chance to limber up my legs on the ascent. Although I climbed skyward with little physical difficulty my mental status encountered an infinitely more vicious assault. I was rapidly shocked into a geriatric renaissance as I watched Jared, so aghast that my mandible bruised the skin over my left kneecap, scamper up the steps like a six legged mountain goat on amphetamines. I am careful to keep in respectable shape. I run, swim and walk regularly, lift weights when available and try to watch what I eat. I admit an occasional penchant for certain adult beverages, particularly those poured on the rocks, from a keg or bottle, or taken straight up. But then again, who climbs stairs with their liver? Jared's singular athletic accomplishment is to maintain an erect posture while taking a shower. His notion of health food is to wash down a pastrami on rye with a chocolate donut and can of Coke. However, when push came to shove, he left me in his wake. I blamed it on the weight accorded all of the peso notes in my wallet, bills that he would have no chance of ever acquiring if he continued to deflate my ego in such a nonchalant manner.

    Once at the summit, we did the requisite "oohing and ahhhing" at the view. We were soon joined by Raphi and then Sharon, whose initial ascents were delayed by a momentary trepidation concerning the dreaded ill-designed stairs. More interesting than the "photo-op" valley below, however, was the sight of a group of aging hippies, in full regalia of sandals, colored beads, cut-off shorts and unkempt coifs, holding a "Sun Ceremony" at the peak. I am not sure where they purchased the scented candles, but I assume one of our friendly native onyx turtle and fifty percent cotton t-shirt merchants had a stash of candles set aside specifically for anyone wearing granny glasses, a "peace sign" headband and flowers in their hair. I am certain we had witnessed neither the first nor the final such solar worshipping congregation of the week. Had we desired to stay for the evening, we most likely could have watched a convoy of Volkswagen Microbuses assemble at the Temple of the Moon at the other end of the archeological site arriving in preparation for the Lunar Observance to follow. Grateful Dead flashlights, anyone? Just fifty pesos.

    The trek up the pyramid afforded me a few moments to ponder the despair of the ancient priests who were destined to mount those same dastardly stairs as a matter of routine, sans well cushioned, ankle supporting Nikes.

Imagine their dedication. The modern Catholic Church can't even stock their diocese with sufficient clergy to adequately service their congregants; and they get to work in flat, air conditioned buildings. I guess the minor issue of celibacy must have something to do with it. The ancient high priests were at least rewarded by the presence of a sacrificial virgin at the completion of their climb. Their contemporary counterparts have only their faith and their desire to uplift humanity to keep them going. Sign me up for a ten story climb with no hand rails, please. Worse than the priest's dilemma, consider the plight of the sacrificial virgin herself. After schlepping the 300-odd steps in the baking heat to the top of the pyramid, she was "rewarded" with the forcible extraction of her still beating heart. So much for our modern medical theories concerning exercise and cardiac health. I guess the gods didn't have time to read the latest scientific journals.

Mom, who admits to having been unable to reach the apex of the Pyramid of the Sun on our previous visit four decades before, trudged up to the top with surprisingly little difficulty—-artificial hip, Medicare card and all. Dad, stubborn as ever not to allow his ailing foot and stenosed spine from limiting his activity, somehow arrived at the top as well. In contrast, Dad looked as though the high priest had returned from the dead and, angered by the sight of such a forlorn trespasser, had painfully extracted the old man's heart and maybe a lung and portion of pancreas at the halfway mark. To add to his discomfort, Dad completed the journey holding tightly to the sixty dollar onyx and marble ceremonial mask he had bought at the base. Of course, he could have waited until after his ascent to purchase the souvenir, but he didn't want to risk the possibility of a monetary collapse, police raid, or sudden onyx embargo during his brief interval on the pyramid that would have imperiled his outstanding bargain. This may come as a shock, but although Dad really is a terrific physician with an extraordinary clinical acumen and infinite breadth of medical knowledge, he does not carry over such skills to the world of finance. Dr. "Smith Barney" he is not. I could not understand why the same entrepreneurs who sold him that trinket, undoubtedly snickering at the sight of the limping, perspiring sucker toting his wares up the pyramid, didn't have the forethought to haul a cooler full of Coronas or Dos Equis to the summit. They could have made a lot more than sixty bucks hawking the brews to us desperate gringos, isolated hundreds of feet above the nearest snack bar.

Speaking of refreshments, we returned to our downtown hotel for lunch. Basically the same buffet stocked with virtually identical dishes as the previous evening. Little enticed me. In contrast, everything appealed to Jared and Raphi. The pyramids had piqued their appetites to new heights, if you ignore the unintended pun. No time for a postprandial siesta, though. We sped off to the National Palace to inspect the famed Diego Rivera mural, depicting the pictorial history of Mexico, painted on the wall of the inner court. Rivera is far from my favorite artist, but he is without question the Michael Jordan of Mexican painting. I imagine to those living south of the border, Michael Jordan is the Diego Rivera of American basketball. What about Babe Ruth? Before the basketball phenom's remarkable career, everyone of merit was compared to Ruth. To us connoisseurs of athletic history, Jordan was the Babe Ruth of hoops. At least, Mr. Ruth, in contrast to his more modern heir to the throne of singular greatness, has retained an adjective honoring his prowess. While few Americans would object to having their monumental exploits described as "Ruthian," not as many of our flag waving, apple pie baking brethren would be happy being

Throw Me Under The Bus...Please

considered "Jordanian." Unless, of course, you are Queen Noor of Jordan, the New York City born, Princeton educated wife of the late King Hussein.

All puns aside, I find Rivera's depictions, in general, to be a bit "cartoonish." They would seem more at home on the editorial page of the Mexico City News than hanging on the wall of a museum or government edifice. On the positive side, his murals were fascinating in their complexity, providing a detailed wordless history of his homeland. Most interesting were the artist's opinions concerning the humanity of his subjects, expressed in part by the beauty, or lack thereof, of their personal appearance. Needless to say, Cortez, the ruthless Spanish Conquistador, who by military force and disdainful chicanery subjugated the Aztecs in the early 16th century, was depicted as a deformed freak. The kids were absolutely enchanted by the historical figures, as we strained to incorporate each into the narrated version of Mexican progress Pepe had provided during the ride back from Teotihuacan. I was proud to be the father of two young men with such an in-depth sense of the past and its relevance to today's complex world. I added my less than expert opinions as they looked for reinforcement validating their notion that the wizened, grey bearded man was indeed Karl Marx and the diminutive individual with the distorted face was the despised Hernando Cortes.

By the time the bus crept across town to the Museum of Archeology, I had reached my limit of Meso-American culture. My feet ached, my neck twinged, and my mind wandered to less intellectual pursuits. In short, I was getting cranky, as if an impetuous child. Once again in contrast to their father, our real boys, bolstered by their naturally inquisitive nature, well-mannered upbringing (thanks to their Mom), and residual calories from the obnoxious buffet lunch, remained enthusiastic and inspired. Each clicked away diligently on his digital camera, a wonderful forethought of their mother's. The digital camera is a marvelous invention. Unlike conventional cameras with their finite supply of film and resulting need for expensive processing, these devices are able to keep Sharon and the kids engaged for hours. They spent the afternoon capturing images of everything in their field of view at little additional expense save for the price of batteries. Since the members of my family, and I assume many other trigger happy individuals, are too lazy to download the photos onto a computer hard drive or to even view them later on the tiny camera screen, most are simply deleted. Therefore, there is no need for the old fashioned ritual of spending the month following a vacation rummaging through underexposed photographs of scenes not worth capturing in the first place, mere days after witnessing them in the flesh, anyway.

I remember the trepidation my siblings and I shared as children, when every mailman's visit in the weeks following a family outing brought another box of 36 color slides, Dad's favored means of image capture. For days on end, we were forced to assemble after dinner in the darkened living room to review the Technicolor spectacle, narrated by Dad's exacting, loquacious monologue. The man who could not find his favorite pair of socks buried in the bottom drawer of his dresser could detail the pertinent last three centuries of municipal history, exact population and average property tax rate for every town he had ever encountered. Mom generally fell asleep, awakening periodically to utter a nonspecific quip under her breath as evidence of her intense interest. We, members of the younger generation, sat restlessly and prayed for a blown projector bulb, case of dinner induced food poisoning or errant 747 plowing into the downstairs bathroom to save us from our fate. Who would have thought that a few decades later, in direct contradiction to this paternally induced "photo-phobia" (get it?), I would

Throw Me Under The Bus...Please

make a career of once again sitting in a darkened room, viewing and describing what are, in essence, just glorified, over-priced black and white vacation pictures? That is, if one were forced to take his or her annual leave in the regional medical center, breathing the ocean air from a respirator and sipping banana daiquiris through a feeding tube. Maybe that's not such a bad idea, in light of our current vacation situation. The food couldn't be any less inspiring.

Interestingly, though, I neither own a camera nor have much desire to snap pictures of my own, regardless of the subject at hand. Then again, few attractive young models have ever asked me to compile a scantily clad spread for their Penthouse audition. Instead, I seem to be a magnet to every camera toting, unnaturally gregarious foreign tourist in need of a family portrait adjacent a site of assumed eternal interest. I have never photographed my own sons, but I am the man behind the lens for a least a dozen staged portraits of Australian, Japanese or German traveling high school orchestras posing on the front steps of the Metropolitan Museum of Art, hot dog in one hand, subway map in the other and foam rubber Statue of Liberty cap tilting laughably on their heads.

The first full day of sightseeing was finally in our wake and yet another buffet dinner awaited us at the hotel. It appeared hauntingly similar to the lunch spread which, as you may recall, bore more than a passing resemblance to the previous evening's repast. However, tonight's meal was touted as a special "Mexican Food Night." No joke. I guess that is like McDonald's celebrating its not-to-be-missed "Hamburger and Fries Day," or sampling a restaurant in Beijing that touted a weekly blue plate offering of "Chinese Food." The double irony was that, once again, very little of the spread appeared particularly Mexican, unless one considers baked ziti and lemon meringue pie washed down with a

Jeffrey A. Miller

Corona as a national staple. I have been to diners in Ohio with a larger selection of south of the border cuisine. I wondered if plopping chocolate pudding on my chicken cutlet could be counted as Mole sauce. Pickled cactus was one of the few attempts at authenticity, although the chevre cheese pairing seemed geographically challenged, to say the least.

V. SUNDAY, DAY THREE: MEXICO CITY TO VERACRUZ VIA PUEBLA

Day three of the tour began with another run in the park and, much to the chagrin of the restless cheeks of my posterior, an even longer stint on the bus. Already, I was stuck in a routine, exactly what I was trying to avoid on vacation. Wake up early for a run in the dark, making sure to stay near the hotel lest I get lost and left behind; arrive back at the room before the unwavering 7am deadline set to have ones bags packed for loading into the bus; a few quick pushups and sit-ups followed by a cursory shower and sprint back down to our dreaded vehicle. Our destination this morning was Puebla, about three hours down the road. Whereas Mexico City had the anonymous hustle of a typical megalopolis, in which everyone, rich and poor, natty or unkempt, rushed through their day with eyes fixed forward and brows cemented in an impenetrable scowl, Pueblo was a jolly city. The streets were clean and the inhabitants all seemed to be enveloped by a cheerful, almost raucous, vibe. I was uncertain whether the citizens were really a merry lot or merely that it was Sunday, the one day off in what was likely, for many, a week of hard physical labor and emotional strife. Regardless, as a tourist, it was a pleasant respite from the austere calm of the ancient ruins to observe peddlers engulfed by a galaxy of fluorescent balloons, stands hawking intricately sliced melons and fruity ices and a circus wagon hauling a family of exotic baboons. As a finishing flourish, the entire scene was framed by rows of centuries old buildings resplendent in a rainbow of ceramic Tala Vera tile.

We stopped briefly at a shop that sold bowls, dishes, platters and tiles fabricated from the town's signature ceramic. It was quite apparent that Pepe frequented the same store, out of dozens of similar merchants on the block, with each of his helplessly captive tour groups. His anticipated appearance was treated with undue graciousness by the proprietors. The greetings resembled those afforded the allied troops in 1944 as they marched down the Champs Elysee after the liberation of Paris. Although I witnessed no actual transfer of paper or coin, a monetary kickback was undoubtedly the driving force behind this arrangement. Once again, we were learning as much about the universality of unregulated, virgin capitalism as about Mexican history. We figured, correctly, as well, that better prices and selection of Tala Vera earthenware were available on the internet. We ordered several intricately patterned serving pieces shortly after we settled back in the US, from a distributor based in Arizona. No bus rides or kickbacks required. Plus, free shipping for orders of fifty dollars or more.

Too bad there was little opportunity to gather more than a cursory glance at the Sunday revelry, as we were promptly herded off in military precision to our appointed lunch destination. Surprise, no buffet, but an actual sit-down establishment with waited service. However, I was more interested in reconnoitering the sites of Puebla than with yet another invitation to dine with the same forty assigned cohorts who, by necessity, had been my companions the past 48 hours. I sat just long enough to suck down half of Sharon's beer and a few taco chips with salsa and guacamole. Nothing spectacular, but several notches fresher than the average American taco

Throw Me Under The Bus...Please

chain. I could only remain in a seated position for so long, as another four hours on the road beckoned. I departed on my own with a stated mission, or more accurately, excuse, of photographing as many buildings decorated in whimsical Tala Vera tile as the short time remaining in Puebla would permit. I know, I have previously admitted to rarely carrying a camera, but a session of amateur photojournalism was the best excuse I could contrive for initiating this private excursion. Besides, I was further prodded to the exit by the cacophony of the incessant mariachi band, blaring their finest brassy cords with a vitality better suited for Yankee Stadium, upper deck. Before I had the opportunity to film more than a couple of tiled structures, we were back on the bus, headed for the port city of Vera Cruz. True to my words, I deleted the pictures promptly after showing my work to Sharon. She was only marginally impressed with my poorly arranged images but was delighted that I had not been run over by any dilapidated station wagons overloaded with inebriated weekend revelers in the process.

The next leg of our journey was endless. Pepe was performing a yeoman's job attempting to entertain us with endless factoids and historical tales. Little, however, could relieve the monotony of mile after mile (or, not to be an ignorant American, kilometer after kilometer) of mountains, volcanoes and sugar cane. Jane Austen afforded little relief, as her narrative seemed as devoid of drama as the arrival of the next rest stop. I turned to a book detailing infamous crimes of the twentieth century and another book depicting abbreviated sports oddities that Sharon had sneaked into my backpack for just such butt-numbing occasions. She knows me well. The one page tales outlined in both volumes were perfect for my Lilliputian attention span. My derriere and lower back were too sore to pay in-depth mental patronage to anything but the pleasant thought of descending the five

Jeffrey A. Miller

narrow stairs adjacent the right front wheel to a blissful patch of terra firma. It mattered little if this were a dirt trail, side walk, gas station parking lot or maximum security penitentiary recreation yard, as long as I could remain upright for a few moments. I never realized the simple act of sitting could be both so mentally and physically agonizing. I attempt to stand and saunter a few rows up and down the isle, much to the dismay of the unfortunate souls seated with their heads adjacent my perspiring buttocks. They should thank me for skipping the rice and beans at lunch and for packing sufficient clean underwear for the entire journey. My increasing irritability has stripped me of any sense of mercy or altruism. Purely out of spite, I dream of ambling the isles of the bus, as a sumo wrestler, sporting only a skimpy leather thong in the crack of my voluminous, oyster stew nourished, "mother-of-all-tushies." In contradiction to my earlier statement concerning wealth and body mass, this is one case in which a vengeful person as myself, although still not too rich, could definitely be too thin.

Speaking of entertainment, or the lack thereof, the monotony of the highway has provided me with a rare opportunity to study Mom and Dad in their element. Vaudeville it is not. Dad, usually rather boisterous and self assured, had been hauntingly subdued by the pain of his foot and lower back. His usually inquisitive persona, never without an obscure query for the tour guide, fellow travelers or men's room attendant, had been silenced by his physical maladies. Although I had spent my life mocking his indefatigable quest for knowledge, whether it concerned the genealogy of the royal family of Dubai or the mineral content analysis of the surface of Venus, I now felt only sympathy for his inward silence. I somehow missed his classic confident, albeit somewhat haughty ability to "correct" even the most learned scholar. Many a tour guide and museum docent has been subjected to his encyclopedic bombardment. Often, believe it or not, he was right. It was the manner of his subtle hubris that would grate the surrounding contingent. My mom, emboldened by her husband's new quiescence and invigorated by her trek to the peak of the Pyramid of the Sun, had herself taken the role of omniscient sage to any captive audience in the vicinity. Unfortunately, her new sense of confidence was directed more towards subjects she knew little about than the multitude in which she is truly expert. Asked about help with legal matters, parent-child relations or even cooking and one is now met with a curt, "You know, it's easy." Thanks, Mom. But query her on the phonetic structure of the Inuit language or the ethnography of the inhabitants of ancient Fiji and its effect upon their political structure and you will be rewarded with a 45 minute dissertation, embellished with personal encounters groomed from prior foreign journeys. Unfortunately, such minor details as names, dates, nationalities and species are confused or forgotten. Sort of like a Wikipedia chapter corroborated by the inebriated members of an elite college fraternity after their freshman rush ceremony but prior to more sober online editing.

    After what appeared to be a millennium shuttling down a nondescript highway, the bus finally rolled toward the vicinity of Vera Cruz. Unfortunately, Pepe implored the driver to take the infamous "scenic route," more appropriately translated from the original Spanish as "longer route," through the outskirts of town. I felt like the clock had been turned back to 1839. I was a Cherokee Indian accompanied by the other members of my tribe and Pepe was Andrew Jackson, forcing us to march the "Trail of Tears" towards Oklahoma. Only, meaning no insensitivity to their horrific plight, the original Native American victims of this heinous act were able to at least stretch their legs during the journey. Every additional nanosecond confined within our mobile penitentiary felt like the length of an aria at a Chinese opera, sung in high pitched Mandarin. While not exactly the physical equivalent of water boarding, I nonetheless maintained the sensation of perpetual agony better reserved for a Sylvester Stallone movie. To make the experience more excruciating, Pepe pointed at row upon row of well groomed, lightly utilized public beaches. Adjacent the requisite palm trees, each beach housed a Corona beer tent just yards away from the softly curling surf. I contemplated smashing a window and leaping from my rolling cell, driven by the setting sun like a hatchling tortoise towards the golden waters to our right. I ruminated too long. We turned from the coast towards the inland hotel. I guess, in retrospect, I am still better off than the average baby turtle, the majority of whom end up as an evening appetizer for a screeching seagull, just yards from the slightly more hospitable ocean. Sadly for the infant plated reptiles, the inviting aquamarine water is far from an impenetrable sanctuary, either. Their flopping little flippers and rounded shells resemble dinner bells both to my complex human imagination as well as in the simple, more focused minds of every large piscine predator in the vicinity. I must admit, from the vantage point of the marauding predatory fish, it beats the hell out of our usual dinner-time buffet.

    The hotel at Vera Cruz was actually quite pleasant. It was a beautifully refurbished older structure in the center of town, reconfigured with the most modern and politically correct amenities. The building had everything from energy saving compact fluorescent lights that automatically dimmed as one left the hallway to low voltage flat screen televisions. The pool, however, seemed an afterthought, seemingly designed for baby seals and penguins rather than six foot hairless humans. It resembled a typical ice cube tray in both physical size and in water temperature. Maybe this was the ultimate environmentally friendly feature. No heat. Little water usage. I counted three strokes to the lap, which was about as much exposure as I could endure, as it was filled with water frigid enough to shrink the pride and joy of the most virile stallion to the size of a birthday party pony's. No need to detail the effects of such an arctic bath on the anatomy of a mere human. Just consider the water spouts of those European fountains of Cupid and his little (in more ways than one) friends. The boys and my father lasted about two laps before retreating to the deck. Mom stayed a few minutes longer, determined to complete at least a small portion of her usual daily swim. Very small. My machismo led me to out-distance Mom by about twelve seconds before the blue complexion of my fingers forced a hasty retreat to shore as well.

Fortunately, the aforementioned threat of frostbite energized my other senses and we were diverted by a festive dance fiesta in the village square across the street. The flowing costumes and precision steps employed by what were virtually the only attractively dressed individuals we had witnessed all week were refreshing. Like a lukewarm margarita, however, the novelty lasted but a few minutes. The music and movements soon became monotonous. Besides, we were warned not to be late for dinner, lest we miss the opportunity to partake in yet another "opulent" native buffet.

Surprisingly, the food was of slightly better quality than in Mexico City, although suspiciously similar in content. The ingredients seemed fresher and, nestled forlornly in an inconspicuous steel chafing dish was the star of the meal, an untitled large white fish poached in a vegetable broth. It was actually worthy of a second helping. Of course, none of the staff could, or more specifically, would, identify the species or even common name of our finned delight. My queries as to its origins were met with similar shoulder shrugs by all in the room and a suspicious depletion of the staff's previously enviable English vocabulary. I reacted to this subterfuge with more than a small share of trepidation, as I imagined only the worst concerning the possible etiology of said large fillet. It may have been garnered from the ornamental fish pond of the hotel down the street or rejected from the cat food cannery on the edge of town. Maybe it wasn't even a fish at all, but the reconstituted innards of a giant Amazonian tree frog or washed up jellyfish. I was certain, though, from my vast knowledge of jungle cookery as gleaned from many a Hollywood B-movie, that it was not derived from a snake. Had it been of serpentine etiology, it would have tasted like chicken, which it did not. The cliché depicting snake, frog legs, nutria and virtually every other non-traditional source of animal protein as tasting like the flesh of a Rhode Island Red has often set me pondering whether chicken really tastes like chicken. Perhaps poultry really resembles iguana meat, which, therefore, should be considered the gold standard of "chickeniness." That must have been the underlying reason why this was the only meal all trip in which we were offered the first beer for free. Better to forget this ridiculous discussion concerning the genealogy of our repast. With a sigh, the brew only reminded me of the aforementioned Corona tents beckoning from the soft warm sand by the glistening Atlantic surf, seemingly light years from our current landlocked location. I downed it and a forty peso companion, anyway.

VI. MONDAY, DAY FOUR: VERACRUZ TO PALENQUE VIA VILLA HERMOSA

The next morning, I had a decent run through the nearly deserted streets of downtown Vera Cruz, a far cry from the pre-dawn bustle of Mexico City. As the streets were set up in a grid, there was little chance of losing my orientation. As per usual, the bus was already full by the 8:00am departure time, with the now anticipated exception of Dad. Our first stop was scheduled to be La Venta Park in Villa Hermosa to see the famed Olmec heads. The eventual destination at some point in the evening, no doubt hundreds of miles down the highway, would be the small village of Palenque. It would serve as ground zero for our immersion into the ruins of the great Mayan civilization.

Pepe did his best to keep us somewhat educated on all facets of Mexican history, both pre and post-Colombian. It was refreshing to hear about the origins and infrastructure of a nation other than our own, especially outside the realm of United States military battles. It has often been stated, not without bit of irony, that the majority of Americans are introduced to foreign geography not through textbooks or formal school lessons but rather via media reports outlining the latest incursion by the US armed forces. This may be true, but after listening to Pepe's detailed dissertation, warfare was undoubtedly the basis of historical orientation south of the border as well. My sons and I find history fascinating in its own accord and even more so when juxtaposed with the past's similarities to the modern world. However, I must admit that the devotion we displayed towards our rolling social studies class was enhanced by the alternative despair of the ceaseless ride. Pepe could have given a sermon on the virtues of penitence and celibacy, in Latin, during such a methodical intercity jaunt and still could have retained the majority of his audience. Nonetheless, *Pride and Prejudice* remained zippered forlornly in my back-pack. No further commentary needed concerning the level of intrigue generated by the Austen novel.

 I shifted from my usual perch adjacent Jared and plopped down next to Mom. She enjoyed conversing about the daily trivialities of the kids lives, but, as I have previously despaired, provided little insight when queried about more difficult or controversial aspects of child rearing. She lost all linguistic capabilities when attempting to discuss such controversial topics as enforcing proper study habits, Raphi's propensity towards snacking and my own trepidation concerning the kids' all too rapid maturation. These were areas in which I had expected Mom to be a sage. Maybe she was but was keeping unusually mum concerning her experiences. I think she might have perceived these to be lessons Sharon and I were better off working out for ourselves. Unusual, given my parents' usual desire to influence all minutia of their children's lives, albeit often in a rather subtle, offhanded fashion. Determined not to leave me totally bereft of information, there was no shortage of verbiage concerning Mom's less than encompassing knowledge of traditional Mexican dance and music. This was accompanied by a few live sample bars of a traditional folk melody which Mom somehow managed to utter in a voice almost identical to a water damaged original Edison cylindrical phonograph recording. It appears that Sharon and I will have to "wing it," left to decipher the secrets of pre-adolescent mentoring on our own. So far, I think we have done a satisfactory job. Then again, they haven't yet learned to drive.

As the bus continued its arduous journey down the highway, I pondered the fate of the B-2 bomber pilots during the initial phases of Operation Enduring Freedom. Regardless of ones views about the budgetary, humanitarian or strategic forethought of flying a two billion dollar stealth aircraft directly from Whiteman Air Force Base, in the heart of Missouri, half way across the world just to drop a couple bombs on a target that was basically devoid of any defenses anyway, my thoughts were on the pilots themselves. The round trip in the subsonic jet took approximately 35 hours and required several aerial refueling procedures. Although I am told the plane can fly safely with only one of its two pilots in the cockpit and there is even a flush toilet on board, the monotony of such a journey must have been astounding. I would have rather flown a Kamikaze mission for the Japanese in the Second World War. At least they were guaranteed of an exhilarating trip, albeit brief. Nonetheless, even the B-2 pilots had a few minutes of excitement, or more correctly, terror channeled into a massive adrenalin rush at the midpoint of the mission when the bombs were deployed. We had no such Edvard Munch "Scream" type event to fortify our spirits. We could only hope that peering at an ancient twenty ton carved stone head, the much heralded highlight of today's excursion to La Venta Park, would at least be moderately novel. As for the on board toilets, given the frequent rest stops, I had little use for the one on the bus. Still in denial that the master bathroom in our house set us back almost $20,000 to only partially remodel, I can only imagine what it cost to construct a useable commode on a federally financed military vehicle. Remember the ire over the $7,600 the US Air force paid for a coffee machine during the late 1980's? The B-2 pilots, if not directing the most harrowing or indispensable mission in the history of modern warfare could at least relish the notion that they were enjoying humanity's most expensive flush.

Speaking of novel, today marked a new concept in vacation dining, one that made us all yearn for the comfort on the previously maligned buffet. We were promised a "box lunch" on the schedule pamphlet. A devilishly misleading statement. An actual grilled or fried cardboard box, as seemingly advertised, would have been much more appetizing. We paused to take what appeared to be a typical rest and refueling break at a truck stop somewhere just west of nowhere. As we departed the vehicle, we were handed a cardboard container holding a white bread, American cheese and mayonnaise sandwich with a bag of chips and a banana. I felt like fourth grade student from Montana, supplied with a meal delicately prepared in the kitchen of the family's trailer home by his 300 pound, tobacco chewing, Oprah watching mother in her K-mart inspired bathrobe. All I needed was a Pabst Blue Ribbon to wash it down, but Dad wouldn't allow drinking until at least the sixth grade. As we have seen, my real Mom has her faults, but, with the exception of the occasional sardine and cream cheese sandwich (don't ask, it was a late 1960's, supposedly upscale thing), lunch was generally a midday treat. Fortunately, at this point in my life, I am not much of a lunch eater, anyway. The unripe banana, probably shipped south from Houston after originating in the Dominican Republic, served me just fine.

Finally, the bus rumbled into La Venta Park. Far from unadulterated or pristine, the park was meticulously manicured with artfully groomed trails and detailed

Throw Me Under The Bus...Please

signage at all points of interest. I wondered when Mickey Mouse would come out of the enchanted castle to shake my hand and sell me a t-shirt. Perhaps, there would be fireworks set to the theme song from *The Lion King* at closing time. Nonetheless, the famed "heads" were impressive. The Olmecs were the predecessors of virtually all of the other major Meso-American civilizations, flourishing just as the Egyptians were dominating Africa and the Middle East. They are best known, however, as the carvers of huge stone heads, weighing as much as twenty tons. These statues have flat-nosed Asian features, which to my minimally trained gaze, appear almost Polynesian. However, in reality their appearance reflects genetic origins derived from Mongolia. It's a small world, after all. Come to think of it, wasn't that an attraction at the original Disneyland? I remember visiting that pavilion as a five year-old. Interesting.

 A diminutive zoo at the end of the trail was, to use Jared's parlance, pretty lame, although the black jaguar it housed was a truly magnificent feline. Its black-on-black spots reminded me of a Paul Klee painting, only much more sensuous. It deserved better than to be imprisoned in a stark steel cage, a remorseful but appropriate bit of garnish to an equally tamed archeological expedition. After our brief trek through the park, it was back to our own rolling shackles for the journey to the little town of Palenque. One glance at our hotel room in this somewhat seedy village, however, and we all yearned to spend the night back in our previously disrespected, but at least tidy, vehicle.

 Although the grounds of the "villa," to use the term loosely, were expansive, they were not particularly ornate or even nominally attractive. A trail snaked behind the two story, sprawling main building, ending at their much vaunted spa. The primary features of this facility included a mud bath, private rooms for massage and an "exercise center" equipped with a rusted, partially dismantled Universal gym and a stationary bicycle circa the Eisenhower administration. The cramped guest rooms were even less inviting, with cobalt blue stucco walls, minuscule covered windows, and a tiny bathroom providing a suitable habitat to numerous multi-legged, winged critters. What the room lacked in traditional accoutrements, it made up for in a colorful, animated menagerie of insects and arachnids of all colors and sizes. The scene reminded us of summers at the Jersey Shore, most specifically a particular establishment on Point Pleasant beach.

    The New Jersey beachfront, although breathtaking in its own right and readily accessible to both New York City and Philadelphia, is cursed with a dearth of full service hotels. Most towns are either comprised of single family homes designed for year round or seasonal occupation that have over the years become increasingly luxurious in scale and appointment, and tacky motels with fetid pools, diminutive rooms and little service beyond ice and hot water. The worst of the lot feature warm ice and cold water. Early in our marriage, Sharon, the boys and I scheduled many a summer extended weekend at these shabby shoreline accommodations with the objective of spending as much time on the beach and boardwalk and as little time in the room as weather would permit. Therefore, our Palenque abode, although half a continent to the southwest, elicited many memories, few of them pleasant. It was appointed in the same cobalt blue stucco and illuminated by similar mailbox-sized opaque windows as the aforementioned site at Point Pleasant. Even worse, the incessant buzzing and biting black flies in the Northeast would be nothing but a light snack for the current menagerie of invertebrates. I remember being forced from our motel one muggy Saturday afternoon on

Throw Me Under The Bus...Please

the Jersey Shore by an infestation of Toyota-sized black flies. The manager argued that they would disappear as soon as the winds shifted from the west, over the bay side of the sandbar that comprised the town, to the east, over the open ocean. He forgot to remind us that such a change in the course of the winds was also a harbinger of brisker, rainy weather. We were left to contemplate the summer vacationer's most feared dilemma. Bugs now versus rain tomorrow. To my chagrin, there was little threat of precipitation in Palenque. I would not have hesitated to trade dripping hair and a pair of soggy sneakers for a few hours devoid of the obnoxious winged Mexican vermin.

Years ago, as we fled that beachfront room in Point Pleasant, NJ, overlooking a littered parking lot, we sought refuge at the Jacuzzi-sized pool, "attractively" set in the midst of an Astroturf deck. We could not actually view the layers of trash outside our window, the detritus of throngs of summer revelers past, as we are not endowed with Superman's "x-ray vision" to peer through the layers of grime caked onto the glazed mail slot that served as a window. This was not just any artificial turf, but a buckled, frayed expanse of dark green petroleum-based vegetation decorated in a haphazard array of rectangular cigarette burns, some still retaining the smoldering tobacco laden culprit. As the proprietor refused to reimburse our visit were we to depart early, I convinced Sharon to spend at least one night at the lodge. My inherent miserly ideations had, at least for one evening, trumped my feelings of revulsion for pathogenic microbes as well as my concerns for the outward health of my family. When we returned to the room, Sharon and I made a desperate dash to the bottle of Makers Mark bourbon stashed in my bag, the better to forget our surroundings. I poured a large glass, actually a plastic cup serving as the Jersey Shore equivalent, added some ice and rested the concoction on the night stand.

Uncharacteristically, Jared had learned to cruise and walk very early in life, fully ambulatory before nine months, as did his younger brother. Proud father that I am, I was certain this was an indication of athletic genius. I was all prepared to address the provost at Notre Dame to reserve two spots in the backfield of their football team before I was forced to despondently accept the notion that this surprisingly early physical prowess had completely tapped their future glycogen reserves. Walking was the last great athletic achievement for either of them, lest we count falling down the stairs without suffering major head trauma a great accomplishment. I had not yet become accustomed to Jared's new propensity to explore spaces above ground level and felt safe depositing my drink unguarded on such a low table. So much for the best laid plans of mice, men and fathers. Before we had realized what had transpired, Jared's face contorted into a quizzical frown, followed by a loud cry. Jared had just "enjoyed" his first alcoholic beverage. The first scotch I ever sampled tasted like iced iodine, replete with an initial lip numbing sting and intrusive metallic aftertaste. I am sure Jared's bourbon left a similar negative imprint on his palette. Needless to say, I felt terrible for my carelessness but, blissfully the boy didn't spill a drop. The delayed reaction of the alcohol slowly imploding his taste buds must have allowed sufficient time to calmly place the cup back on the table before the release of the full, astringent ethanol burst. My son.

Speaking of punishing ones taste buds, tonight's buffet made the spreads at the prior two hotels resemble the wedding of Charles and Dianna, both in opulence and gastronomic quality. The monstrous open air cafeteria reminded me of chow time in elementary school, only there was no separate ice cream line to substitute for the barely palatable main courses. The raucous multinational crowd, primarily German, added to the soccer stadium ambience. I looked for the classic #48 cans of sodden vegetables and plaster-based turkey stew. At least those classics of culinary assault were, by definition, sterilized during the canning process. Lord knows the background of the floating morsels scattered about the steam table. To enhance the wedding-from-hell atmosphere of the meal, a stuperous band pounded out old Broadway show tunes at a decibel level befitting a Green Bay Packers' playoff triumph at Lambeau Field. They were so cacophonous that not even the Germans, crowded into a tropical facsimile of a Beer Garden after a buffalo stampede, could bring themselves to sing along.

VII. TUESDAY, DAY 5: PALENQUE ALL DAY

As we discovered the next morning, the one positive feature of our villa was its proximity to the Palenque archeological site. Joyfully, we had a rare day spent predominantly on our feet rather than our derrieres. The village itself had a third world authenticity not present in our previous travels. It was a hilly amalgam of cramped apartments, ramshackle homes and lightly frequented shops. The town square, however, was clean and well maintained, crowded with locals playing cards, selling snacks or just relaxing. It was the type of Mexican village often stereotyped in the popular media, mangy dogs, wandering chickens and all. I could picture Warner Brothers' Speedy Gonzalez darting through the center square, grabbing cheese niblets from a series of strategically located spring loaded mouse traps, all the while chased by a mustachioed, bandolier wearing, revolver toting, feline bandito; or Walt Disney's Goofy dog snoozing under a cactus, sombrero tilted over his eyes and rainbow striped poncho rolling up and down his chest with each snoring breath. Of course, this being the 21st century, there were numerous merchants, conversing in quite comprehensible English, selling t-shirts, plastic Mayan pyramids and packaged potato chips. We made it our business to buy a bag of Frito's Corn Chips,

Throw Me Under The Bus...Please

interestingly flavored with a hint of lime. Our best meal in Palenque.

Palenque was our first immersion into Mayan architecture, comprised of stone temples, residences of the nobility and pyramids. Although occupied since about 500AD, it had its heyday in the seventh century when it was the center of Mayan culture and religion. Palenque remained hidden in the tropical jungle until 1952, long after it was abandoned by its original inhabitants in the tenth century. The pyramids were used as both promiscuous bases for their temples and as tombs for the royalty buried beneath. One edifice even housed three stone commodes which, not surprisingly, looked just like modern toilets only constructed of chiseled stone rather than porcelain. They even "flushed," as the expelled waste dropped into a stream conveniently running beneath the governor's quarters. Sorry ladies, but the Mayan men had a great excuse for not lifting the seat when they had to "go." It was just too damn heavy. I don't know whether his longevity was due to the modern sanitary facilities or the exercise afforded by the seemingly endless stairs awaiting a simple trip to temple for afternoon prayer or human sacrifice, but King Pacal, Palenque's most influential emperor, ruled from 620–684AD. Very unusual for the day, he lived to see his eightieth birthday. That makes former King Hali Salasi of Ethiopia appear to have been a mere transient.

Pacal is most noted in our modern culture for the hieroglyph, inscribed in dark red dye on the front of his stone sarcophagus, depicting him rising towards the heavens after his demise. This image was turned sideways and reproduced in the popular 1968 book by Erich Von Daniken about alien influence on human civilizations, *Chariots of the Gods*. It was claimed to depict the king wearing a helmet and space suit, cruising through cosmos seated in a rocket in a manner mimicking a Mercury astronaut centuries later. Such claims of extraterrestrial influence on ancient Meso-American culture have generally been debunked, but Jared, in particular, was quite amused nonetheless. Jared prides himself on being somewhat of a junior scholar on UFO's. He is particularly enraptured by the arguments surrounding the supposed aliens found by the US government in Roswell, NM and purportedly hidden in the ultra classified "Area 51." This was as close as he had ever come in real life to an artifact of an alien conspiracy theory. Needless to say, we forked over 250 pesos for a large reproduction of that image of Pacal, burned on a thin sheet of parchment by a local native entrepreneur. It is now hanging, sideways of course, on the living room wall of our Manhattan apartment. It is a fitting decoration, as some of our neighbors in the Clinton (formerly "Hell's Kitchen") section of Manhattan appear as if they had recently escaped from Area 51, themselves.

Once again, we are all awed by Jared's stair climbing facility. At home, he claims his feet hurt and chest aches simply from ambling across the street to the neighbor's house. My request for help mowing the lawn results in a labored bout of coughing and wheezing and, after much prodding, a job performed so superficially that the grass actually appears longer after he is finished than before he sets out. Needless to say, before the mower's engine has had a chance to cool, Jared shoves his open palm towards my gut, demanding his monetary compensation for a job not-so-well done. Maybe it's the dry Mexican air paired with the adventure of reconstituting the steps of long since deceased priests and warriors, but somehow he manages to bound up the stairs of the various Mayan pyramids in the manner of a gazelle chased by a pack of famished lions. I try to keep pace, but soon fall back, resembling a four pack-a-day smoker midway through the Boston Marathon. I blame it on the fumes of the bus exhaust. Raphi, usually the more competitive of the two, is once again, as in Teotihuacan, slowed by his fear of heights. Raphi is inherently risk averse, a wonderful feature for a child to maintain. That is, unless as a parent, one enjoys spending evenings consoling a bruised and bloodied child at the nearest emergency room.

Finally, I thought to myself, I could parlay Raphi's caution into a victory for my own downtrodden ego, increasingly deflated by the unavoidably enhanced athletic prowess of my rapidly growing sons. I had out-climbed the lass. However, before I could revel in the thrashing I had handed my younger child on our morning pyramid ascents, he dived in after me as I swam laps that afternoon in the hotel's large but rather murky pool. True to form, it was essentially a larger version of the aforementioned squalid Jersey Shore aquatic facility, sans artificial turf. Instead, bare chipped cement served as the deck surface. Raphi made me appear as a rickety heating oil barge mistakenly meandering through a hydrofoil race course. Obviously, I was slowed by the cold water. Raphi, the child who wears sandals and, at most, a light sweatshirt, even during a January snow, was impervious to that arctic aquatic environment. I was also fatigued, I surmised, as I had skipped the lunch buffet to swim a few serious laps before Raphi, never one to skip a meal, had joined me in the pool. Although the pool's abundance of unidentifiable floating and submerged detritus was a little off-putting, this had been the first real aquatic exercise I had experienced all trip. We would have had more occasions to frolic in the water had we vacationed in Cleveland rather than in this tropical paradise. Something to suggest for our next vacation. Rock and Roll Hall of Fame, a top notch art museum, a Cavaliers' basketball game and unlimited time watching the snow from the heated indoor hotel pool. No buffet and no buses. When is the next flight to Ohio?

Jeffrey A. Miller

After we had completed our morning tour of Palenque's sites, terminating in a modern air conditioned museum containing, amongst other items, Pacal's famed stone coffin and reproduction of the surrounding tomb, our group, like a pack of camera wielding lemmings, headed back to the bus for the thankfully short ride back to the village. Unfortunately, Pepe's quick head count yielded one rapidly balding cranium missing in action. To no one's surprise, it was Dad. We waited 15 minutes, reaping havoc on Pepe's atomic clock inspired schedule. Our guide threatened to leave without said delinquent passenger. I convinced him to provide me five more minutes to reconnoiter the premises for any signs of a limping, perspiring American in a yellow t-shirt. This was the second such incident involving my old man, and the throngs in the vehicle were clearly in favor of letting him find his own mode of transportation back to the villa. Mom, always ready to kick a little extra sand in the eyes of her fallen mate and fearful at being disparaged in unison for being his wife, denied any knowledge of his existence. I think she even removed her wedding band for effect.

I scrambled towards the museum realizing that my seemingly noble act was being viewed with disdain by the other, more punctual, members of the tour. They wanted to teach Dad a lesson but were too polite, or more precisely, too meek to openly voice their opinions. However, the "deafening" whispers and wrinkled foreheads were obvious indications of our comrades' desires. Their ire, however, evoked in me a personal desire to defend the Miller family honor, what little we had. I relished the possibility of being considered a traitor for abetting their enemy. Dad would always be my father. I was burdened with the responsibility of carrying on his genes. He had defended me, at least outwardly, when I had wronged as a child. Of course, an hour in solitary

Throw Me Under The Bus...Please

confinement in my room as punishment for my transgressions would often follow once we were back in private. In contrast, heeding to the influences of my latent Asberger's tendencies, the extra familial members of the tour and their desire for an expedient return to the hotel meant little to me. The boys supported my brief quest to find Dad, and Jared even began to chase after me. He abruptly stopped, however, when he realized it might involve further exertion and worse, could make him late for lunch. Fortunately for all, Dad was spotted heading towards the bus just as I departed, oblivious to the commotion and turmoil on board. Mom said nothing. She opened a book and stared resolutely at the pages. The bus pulled out, as we awaited our first and only unscheduled afternoon of the tour. True to form, it rained.

After our previously described, surreptitiously competitive swim, we headed into the town of Palenque. The village appeared just as forlorn in the relative light of the afternoon as it had during my run in the dark of the early morning. We bought a few trinkets and hunted for allergy medications for Raphi, to no avail. What were advertised as apothecaries displayed a very limited range of recognizable medications, most of which were over-the-counter. The natives appeared to have been conditioned to the arrogance of foreign tourists, but, unless trying to sell us souvenirs, kept primarily to themselves. A glance towards a merchant's wares, however, evoked an instantaneous smile and a few hurried sentences, in perfectly comprehensible English, concerning the relative quality of his merchandise in comparison to his peers. The villagers (Palenqueans?) seemed resolved at the notion that they needed us to maintain the tourist economy that served as the only industry in town. With that dismal view of rural Mexican existence in mind, I found our one afternoon devoid of a specific site to explore more depressing than relaxing or adventurous. The bus didn't seem so bad after all. Why we couldn't have been offered a free afternoon at the beach in Vera Cruz, I will never know. That Corona tent on the tropical shore seemed just a bit more inviting than the pack of mangy dogs chasing screeching chickens and dodging quarter century old Chevy pickups on Palenque's drab main drag.

We have had a continuing joke in my family about my father as "Trivia Champion of the World." It was always meant more as a compliment than derogatory term in the knowledge-obsessed Miller clan. He always had a feasible sounding answer to any question. As I aged, I realized that although an enviable percentage of his responses were correct, many were not. He just amalgamated any associated precepts he may already have maintained and improvised a realistic appearing yarn. When I became a father, with my own inquisitive young boys, I mimicked his technique to derive my own dubiously respectable answers to their queries. However, Pepe made us both appear about as intelligent as two earthworms, lost in the relative complexity of a T-shaped maze, befuddled by the choice of moist dirt versus decaying leaves. Pepe was an indefatigable source of factoids, ranging from the expected, such as Mexican culture and history, to the bizarre, for instance, the corporate structure of the hilariously named "Bimbo Bread Company." Needless to say, Sharon could not leave Mexico before procuring a t-shirt with the company logo. I think Pepe, too, utilized Dad's technique of fabricating answers from bits of related knowledge whenever the question at hand was beyond his primary grasp.

One of his most fascinating tales, told as a direct response to a question on the bus, involved the origin of the ubiquitous, at least in the US toddler birthday party circuit, piñata. He expounded on its origins in China and its introduction to Europe by Marco Polo (natch!).

Throw Me Under The Bus...Please

Understand, in the factoid circuit, China is the nation from which virtually all major developments, technological breakthroughs and common twenty first century items appear to have first evolved. The piñata was originally used in western religious ceremonies, shaped as a seven-pointed star representing the seven moral sins. A following query concerning the genealogy of the Chihuahua dog also attributed origins to China. Although suspicious, I never bothered to back check the accuracy of his responses. Fortunately, his answer to a question about the assassination of Zampata and Poncho Villa never strayed from the America's. Had he mentioned that they hired Chinese mercenaries for their forces, or were disposed of by Asian masters of the martial arts, I would have been forced to call Pepe's bluff.

I am not sure why crowning China as the country of origin for every major development and invention has become such classic slight of hand of the trivia professional. Maybe it is because the nation comprises a quarter of the world's population. By shear mathematics, 25% of all human thought and its productivity is bound to come from the land behind the Great Wall. Did they invent the concept of the wall as well? Gunpowder, the compass, mechanical printing, pasta, karate, rocket propulsion, General Tsao's Chicken, you name it; all are proclaimed to have originated in China. It is kind of like invoking God when discussing the origins of mankind when addressing a rally of The Young Christian Conservative Society or dropping Mick Jagger's name when discussing the paternal lineage of virtually anyone between the ages of six months and fifty years. You can't miss. Ironically, one of the few modern popular items not native to China is chop suey. A favorite dish of many an Asian fast food restaurant, it was developed in America by Chinese immigrant chefs as a means of more

63

Jeffrey A. Miller

efficiently utilizing any edible odds and ends in a manner appetizing to the unsophisticated local palates.

We headed back to the villa after our walk through the town of Palenque for a couple of rounds of cheap tequila served in plastic cups. We finally had time for pre-dinner cocktails, which were poured more out of necessity, to obscure the vermin infested surroundings, than out of pleasure. I may seem like a snob, but no alcoholic beverage, even beer, can be savored in a plastic or paper cup. I like the experience of thick glass, even if it is the glass of the bottle. I also like distilled spirits on the rocks, making it difficult to drink them straight from the bottle. Another forgettable buffet dinner followed, virtually indistinguishable from the prior evening's cruelly satirical facsimile of a working class wedding at a small town German pool hall.

VIII. WEDNESDAY, DAY 6: PALENQUE TO MERIDA VIA UXMAL

The next morning, day six, started out in the usual fashion with an early morning run, a few pushups and arm curls with my red elastic bands, a quick shower, and a rush to the bus for yet another interminable journey down a nameless Mexican highway. The epitome of the term, "Hurry up and wait." The bus rumbled by miles, or should I say kilometers, of pristine Gulf beaches and aquamarine water. Yet another unreachable temptation en route to the next assemblage of moss covered stone pyramids and gift shops replete with plastic facsimiles of, you guessed it, moss covered stone pyramids. Maybe they should sell plastic replicas of the gift shops as well, in the name of authenticity. Why would one desire to purchase a replica of the same ancient structure he or she had just spent the past four hours inspecting and photographing? At that point in time, I, for one, would rather buy a miniature Empire State Building to remind me of home or a shining little Eiffel Tower to hearken the more sophisticated wonders I am missing by tromping around the steamy Mexican jungle looking at piles of retouched rocks. I hope that in the distant future, our descendents will have the wherewithal and sense of humor to line the virtual shelves of their cyber gift shops with stone facsimiles of some of our current plastic structures. For example a stone key chain in the shape of an Aqua Fina bottle. That is, if there is any need for keys in the generations to be. Better yet, how about a large stone re-creation of an early 21st century plastic snow globe depicting a typical moss covered Mayan pyramid. Consider it reversed reverse engineering. One could climb around said structure and simultaneously enjoy the culture of both our current population and the ancient world, all the while cooled being by artificial snow.

I know I have mentioned this previously, but once again I prayed that just once, we could forego another buffet or cutesy "authentic Mexican" restaurant and park the bus at a beach for an hour of tasty waves and tastier Dos Equis. No such luck. After an entire morning spent cocooned by the unfaltering drone of a well tuned diesel engine and endless charcoal grey of the regional highway, we finally pulled into a wooden, surprisingly dark restaurant perched on stilts above a perfectly calm stretch of cobalt blue sea. I tried to linger by the bus, enjoying my first taste of direct solar radiation of the day but soon was whisked into the sullen, nearly empty establishment. Why anyone would design a seaside eatery with no windows to expose the radiant sunshine and adjoining ocean is a mystery. We sat on wooden benches and ordered from our choice of grilled native shrimp or fish. Yes, just "fish." No proper noun. No adjective. Yet another nameless piscine variant, a continuation of the previously lamented national joke on us gringos. The chef's cousin probably worked at the hotel buffet in Vera Cruz, where we had last sampled that surprisingly delectable but sadly nameless inhabitant of the deep. How does the chef know what to ask for when he sets out to purchase our anonymous finned friend? How does the fishmonger advertise the price? What kind of bait does one use to catch such a creature?

When they finally arrived, the shrimp actually had a respectable briny flavor and a meaty texture, features lacking in the crustaceans found in most American restaurants, imported from the aquatic farms of Vietnam. Alas, all was not perfect in the state of Mexico. As I mouthed the second one, although rich in texture, I noted a definite undertone of iodine. This was an ominous sign in a land where Pepto Bismol is considered a traveler's staple to be packed along with ones passport, underwear and walking shoes. I took this as a cue to excuse myself from the table to stretch my toes on a twenty minute jaunt along the shoreline walkway. As I arose, with table manners groomed from a distant past of dining in the most deviant of New England small college fraternity houses, I forked a sample of Raphi's anonymous fish du jour. Needless to say, it was delicious. Unquestionably, the most exquisite morsel I had tasted all trip. Woe is me. I am now cursed, destined to spend the rest of my life scouring fishmongers and seafood restaurants throughout the world in a fruitless mission to once again experience a sample of that exquisite "just fish." Captain Ahab had an easier task.

If one ignored the highway abutting the north side of the sidewalk, the shore adjacent the south side resembled the cover page of a travel magazine. Small fishing craft bobbed aimlessly on a turquoise Gulf (I'm running out of synonyms to describe the color of the tropical sea) under a brilliant, energizing sun. Only, it was but a seaside mirage. Before I could remove my shoes and dip my toes into the aquatic panorama, we were escorted back aboard the sterile confines of the shining silver bus, destined to lose yet another afternoon barreling along a nameless stretch of blacktop. I felt envious of the two young fishermen, almost fully immersed as they attempted to repair to the bottom of their dilapidated white boat. At least they were spending their afternoon in the cooling sea. I would have volunteered to hand them a wrench, but retreated as I contemplated the discomfort involved with spending the next three hours wearing saline laden underwear in my air conditioned seat.

    We finally arrived at Uxmal. It was either the best preserved, or more likely, most carefully recreated site we had yet visited. After having spent so much of the day in a seated position, I was too fidgety by the time we assembled at the park to pay much attention to Pepe's typically informative spiel concerning our new surroundings. I detoured multiple times from the demarcated path to sample the view from the top of as many pyramids as possible. I did this less to witness the scenery than as a desperate attempt to reinstate some circulation to my cramped lower extremities. A million years from now, if these bus tours continue to increase in popularity, people will be born without legs, but instead with oversized bottoms, an extra set of eyes and ears and a triple sized bladder, the better to function in their capacity as passive world travelers. Pepe soon let us in on the secret as to why Uxmal appeared so well mended. President Bush had attended a conference in the area a few years earlier and announced his desire to visit the Mayan ruins of Uxmal. Therefore, by order of the Secret Service, the hosts were directed to level and smooth the stairs and walkways of the pyramids and temples to guard against any potentially embarrassing accidents by the leader of the free world. No one wanted a repeat Gerry Ford "Super-Klutz" scenario. Mr. Bush had become quite adept making a fool of himself without the need for an injurious spill on ancient stones.

    The bus eventually rumbled into the city of Merida at 7:20pm. Dinner, which was to be our first conventional waited, sit-down meal in a hotel, was scheduled to be served ten minutes later. Most members of our group were already seated at their tables by 7:25pm. A more mischievous, fun-loving group of travel mates I could not imagine outside of a cloistered monastery or medieval

Throw Me Under The Bus...Please

convent. In an act of self preservation, I arranged with the maitre d' to make sure our dinner would be held until at least 8:00pm. No pesos were exchanged. My half-exasperated, but fully malignant appearing demeanor sufficed well enough, aided by a subtle confabulation about needing a few extra minutes to call my short tempered boss in Sicily before he dispatched his associates to the hotel to find me. We all prefer some time to shower, unpack and get settled before dining. In case you haven't guessed, "get settled" is a euphemism for "have a shot of tequila and use the john." As feared, that iodine undertone in the shrimp was a sign of early microbial invasion which had now allied with Montezuma's ghost to exact intestinal revenge on yet another ill prepared tourist.

We would have been much better off missing the assigned repast and finding a nearby restaurant. The lack of a buffet table and addition of a waiter translated into a meal without choices. Dinner consisted of classic institutional "rubber chicken" with cold rice and a gelatinous sweetened brown sauce, origin unknown. I think the waiter referred to the gravy in Spanish as, "Mole." My Jewish American palate translated it into the Yiddish as, "Oi vey!" All we needed was a disinterested jazz-pop ensemble and Uncle Herman from Hoboken to cut the cake, and we could have been at any number of wedding receptions, bar mitzvahs or retirement parties across the fifty states. Add a couple of handshakes, balloons and self gratifying speeches, and voila, instant political fund-raiser. Offer the same poultry and accompaniments while raffling off a high definition TV or weekend in Las Vegas and we have arranged the financial backing for the girls junior high field hockey team's annual trip to their tournament in Syracuse. I sure hope some chef, experimenting in the Waldorf Astoria test kitchen years ago, patented this universally uninspired chicken concoction. He would undoubtedly be a millionaire by now.

Dad came to dinner in the same yellow "White Water Rafting" T-shirt he had already worn on three prior days of the tour. He had been alternating daily with a green "Conservation Society" top. Maybe he thought no one else would notice, although his suspicions may have been piqued by the dearth of companions stationed in the surrounding seats on the bus or dinner table. Even Mom seemed to seek excuses to alter her seating arrangement, and she had experienced a half century of Dad's traveling rituals. Although at home, he wore fresh clothing each day and changed upon returning from work, the act of foreign travel seemed to evoke a latent depression-era mentality from the depths of his mind. These were very distant synapses, to be sure, as he was born shortly after the depression had largely run its course. Maybe it was his childhood spent in Brooklyn as the son of a relatively indigent immigrant tailor. Dad had always been proud of how little he could pack. He toted a single carry-on as an over-stuffed badge of honor, even if it meant sending the bomb sniffing dogs at the airport into convulsions.

Dad's ego was further wounded when upon our arrival in Merida, he suggested to Pepe, speaking unsolicited "for the group," that our guide forego the usual 6am wake up call the next morning. Dad was hastily over-ruled, not only by Pepe, but by every other member of the tour, including Mom. Dad's plea was doomed from the outset, as he was the only participant who was ever late in the morning, anyway, phone call or not. I am sure Captain Bligh faced similar difficulties garnering support from his crew as he attempted to convince them of the lenient discipline and tranquil working conditions on board the HMS Bounty. Let them eat Breadfruit! Alas, it is a good thing God is both omniscient and is blessed with an ironic sense of humor. As punishment for Dad's

Throw Me Under The Bus...Please

hubris, the Lord, or perhaps the interior designer, had the foresight to ensure that the hotel was not equipped with room clocks.

The hotel was situated in the center of the city, in a rather busy intersection of narrow crowded streets. Fortunately, the small town square was only a few blocks away. This served as my running track for our two mornings in Merida. The square was small, so a run constituted of about twenty monotonous laps, accompanied by the cacophonous songs of a menagerie of tropical birds. The screeching was so loud and unceasing as to drown out the engine noise from the fleet of buses lining the periphery of the square, awaiting a bevy of sauntering, none-too-harried passengers. One such vehicle took nearly an hour to fill before departing on its daily run. If this was the pace of the commuter transit system at rush hour, one could only imagine the wait for the departure of the community center shuttle from the local retirement home. Perhaps Dad should consider moving to Merida. For once in his life, he would be considered punctual.

While Pepe enjoyed a Margarita at the hotel bar after handing us off to Miguel, our guide du jour, we headed off to the Mayan and Toltec ruins of Chichen Itza. Miguel was initially a bit stiff, although informative. However, in contrast to Pepe, he was no roving Random House but managed to provide an admirable rendition of the intricacies of the Mayan pyramids, temples and Mexico's largest ancient ball field. The Meso-American indigenous people competed in a fascinating sport employing two teams of seven members each. The players utilized a hi-alai type of wicker scoop to propel a six pound rubber ball through a vertically positioned hoop suspended twenty feet in the air at the field's midpoint. The stadium was surrounded by a 25 foot high wall upon which the spectators, all either religious figures or members of the nobility, could sit. We were told that their clapping was amplified in a specific pattern by the dynamics of the sheer stone stadium walls. Miguel ably demonstrated this acoustic anomaly. Interesting sound effects but did they really clap like a stadium full of inebriated Major League baseball fans? Did the ancient Mayans "boo" at a bad call by the umpire? Could one still purchase beer after the seventh inning in those days? The match was in actuality a religious device, not a competition in the western, Olympic or NFL sense. Therefore, the best player on the winning team, all of whom were priests (i.e. the MVP or Most Valuable Priest), would have the dubious "honor" of having his head lopped off as an offering to the gods after the game. And we thought Alex Rodriguez faced undue duress over his on-field performance. In summary, the match appeared to resemble the NBA meets *Mad Max* played in the Roman Coliseum. In Hollywood, however, the writers would have dreamed up a scenario in which Mel Gibson could have evaded the executioner's dagger.

Lunch was at a beautifully restored former Hacienda, now a resort, consisting of linked villas and restaurants, floral lined walkways and multiple pools. A hacienda is basically the Mexican version of a plantation—- a self-contained fiefdom centered by a large farm. The Mexican rendition of pasta primavera, the only main course on the menu, was no match for the lush, inviting surroundings. Why every meal had to contain some version of pasta (those damn inventive Chinese again) and was invariably accompanied by a medley of New Jersey's most readily obtainable winter vegetables, including over-steamed broccoli and cauliflower florets, sliced carrots and minced onion, was beyond me. Worse, the tastiest of the native veggies are shipped to the Northeast US, leaving the dregs for the local establishments.

Once again, in what has become a recurrent theme to this story, I had to battle my innate desire to run back to

Throw Me Under The Bus...Please

the bus, don my omnipresent bathing suit and dive into the deserted 25 meter pool situated behind the restaurant. Instead, I took a quick jaunt around the spectacular grounds, endowed with a series of lazy concrete trails meandering through lush tropical flora. In so doing, I skipped the cocoanut ice cream desert. As you may have guessed, I love cocoanut ice cream, an item difficult to purchase at our local supermarket. In fact, the only other time I had ever visited Mexico, as a six year-old child, we spent three days in Acapulco. All I remember of that trip were the fearless cliff divers, swimming around the hotel pool in the searing afternoon heat and topping off every meal with a bowl of the most luscious cocoanut ice cream. Nonetheless, I convinced myself that my stroll through the gardens endowed more visceral fortitude upon my soul and my feet than any mere frozen concoction could provide decadent pleasure for my tongue.

By this point in the tour, the creases of my brain (sulci, to the more medically initiated) had been crammed with more minutia concerning pre-Columbian Aztec, Olmec, Toltec and Mayan culture than any modern human being or even computer server could ever wish to retain. It reminded me of my many, more precisely, far too many, years as a student. During that time, I was always cognizant that virtually everything I had garnered so much effort remembering for the final exam would be wiped clean from my grey matter before my pencil had returned to my pocket. Just like a distressed student as well, I still yearned for a "real" vacation, learning nothing more than the difference between a strawberry margarita, strawberry mojito and strawberry daiquiri. This primal desire for unadulterated pleasure was unabated by the realization that most of the archeological sites we had visited had long since become "cultural Disneyworlds," as Sharon so aptly described them, replete with appropriate

Jeffrey A. Miller

t-shirts, refrigerator magnets, ice cream stands and "Keep Off!" signs in Spanish, English, German, French and Japanese. Although I now possess a few more factoids under my belt, suitable only for use in the next unofficial trivia contest, I have gathered nothing about the actual experience of ancient aboriginal life. That is, unless I equate the anguish of our many interminable hours on the bus with the brutality of being disemboweled by the sharp knife of a paint and bead adorned pagan high priest. I might just choose the blade. It is quicker and less painful, albeit a bit messier on the upholstery.

Unlike the US model, the Mexican government and, I assume, the entire national psyche, emphasize the monumental contribution of the nation's indigenous heritage towards the development of their contemporary society. This, in part, may be due to the large proportion of the current populace retaining native bloodlines, estimated at over 50%. We Americans, in contrast, would rather bury our aboriginal past, instead emphasizing the role of immigration from foreign lands in creating the diversity and strength of our nation. We seem to envision our sophisticated modern culture as the result of a victory by our diverse, forward thinking, upwardly mobile European descendant over the stagnant, insular native populations. Americans consider the evolution of science and culture as purely European concepts, tenets not present in the genome of any other races or ethnic groups. Remember the myriad of contributions of the Chinese we discussed earlier? In the West, all the credit goes to Marco Polo for having the forethought, or more likely entrepreneurial spirit, to import said inventions back to Europe. What of the technological and architectural advances of the ancient Meso-Americans? They must have been copied from visiting aliens from another galaxy. Alas, I am beginning to play with fire. Being of European descent myself, albeit of the more lowly

Eastern European stock, I will abruptly end my dissertation on the politics of race and culture and continue with a less controversial but equally universal concept. Let's go shopping!

IX. THURSDAY, DAY SEVEN: MERIDA TO CHICHEN ITZA

Chichen Itza was particularly chock-a-block with virtually identical Mayan vendors, many of whom sold exquisite, colorfully glazed ceramic dishes, trays and bowls. Some displayed more traditional Mayan designs but most had very colorful post revolutionary themes. We bought several pieces, the perfect authentic-looking accoutrement for the necessary NFL half time refreshments of "Nacho Cheese" Doritos and medium spicy salsa from a jar. If nothing else, a bag of Fritos served in a folk art bowl is closer to traditional meso-American fare than a plate of spaghetti and cheese on iceberg salad served to a group of German tourists at our typical hotel buffet.

As we amble through our final archeological site, I remain in awe of the boys' exceptional behavior. They have remained interested in both the local culture and the historical background. They are friendly and courteous to everyone in our group and respectful of the diligent entrepreneurs running the souvenir stands. In turn, they have been rewarded with a rare travel experience, quality time with their grandparents and, most significantly, a trunk full of Mexican knick-knacks, chatchkis and coins. Their haul ranges from black obsidian daggers to plastic replicas of a Toltec head dress; Olmec head t-shirts to a sombrero-clad rubber duck bath toy; a bag of lime-

Throw Me Under The Bus...Please

flavored Frito chips printed in Spanish to the grey feather of some native species of bird found on the roadside. Surprisingly, not a single Mayan-pyramid snow-globe paperweight was to be found. The Japanese tourists must have snatched them all up the previous week. Thankfully, we deferred on the vinyl blow-up black jaguar that squeaked like an asthmatic adolescent when one squeezed its tail. How much of this booty will ever make it out of the suitcase is debatable, but that is insignificant. A mind full of memories is worth infinitely more than a shelf full of souvenirs. At least until years later when one attempts to discard some the long forgotten items and is met with a tantrum and Niagara Falls of tears. In a much more superficial sense, this is similar to the old aunt who one never finds the time to visit but leaves an inescapable emotional void when she is finally gone. So please, get in the car and pay ol' Aunt Edna a brief social call. She may even give you an old trinket to remember her by. Perhaps a snow-globe paperweight of the Empire State Building purchased when she came to New York for your Bar Mitzvah.

Sharon unwittingly inherited the Sisyphean task of not only keeping her sons content and safe in a foreign land, but also of acting as her husband's advocate in the face of often adverse surroundings. Not the physical environment of crowded archeological ruins, ever changing hotel rooms, filthy rest stops and cramped vehicle seats. She knows, persistent complaining aside, I could handle such minor discomforts on my own. Instead, Sharon was my emotional savior during our week long ordeal, an unflappable barrier planted firmly between my parents' desire to retain long deferred domination over their oldest son and my own, often self destructive, obstinacy. She knows when to take my hand when I am uptight; how to remove the anxiety of planning and packing; and the utility of slipping me a shot of tequila when I am over the edge. Most uniquely, she can sense when I need to be alone, be it to ponder, pout, or just wander. She manages to keep herself, and more importantly, the rest of my beloved family at a reasonable distance during these moments. Unlike me, she always eschews the outward appearance of having a good time and manages to concentrate on the pleasurable aspects of every experience, rather than perseverate on the more odious ones, as I tend to do.

Payback, of course, arises on occasion when we are alone and her suppressed negative aura is unleashed, generally without warning or specific inciting event, towards her designated, legally committed punching bag. At these times, I try to say little, drink a lot, and await the arrival of the Sandman to whom Sharon, in general, quickly succumbs. The next morning, all is forgotten, the slumber having exorcised the daemons for the time being. Nonetheless, these occasional bouts of venom are a small price to pay for the many hours of devotion and sanity Sharon provides. I guess a simple bouquet of flowers or fancy dinner cannot adequately display my appreciation. I wish I had purchased that glow-in-the dark refrigerator magnet of Diego Rivera mocking Sr. Cortez while we were in Mexico City. Fortunately, Sharon truly seemed to be having an enjoyable vacation, infatuated by the history and architecture and thankful for the time on the bus to read, uninterrupted by phone calls, school meetings and dinner preparation. For Sharon, the chance to linger in sunny, warm surroundings in the middle of February is a reward unto itself. I think I have just convinced myself that no gifts are necessary.

We returned to our hotel in Merida after yet one more interstellar omnibus journey. There was just enough time on the clock before dinner to paddle off of few laps in the pool. Once again, I was quite disheartened to discover that the water was piped directly from the Arctic Sea,

Throw Me Under The Bus...Please

with a quick detour through the flooring of the hotel's walk-in freezer. Along with the delectable unnamed baked fish and the dreary buffet dinner, this penchant for frigid pool water has proven to be a running joke throughout the Mexican hospitality industry. I am not sure where the lodge management found such frigid water in a tropical local where the ambient temperature never sees the south side of 80 degrees. I am also befuddled by their rationale. Perhaps, the staff figured it would be easier to keep the pool clean if no one ever used it. Maybe, they were planning to assemble a penguin exhibit for the viewing pleasure of their guests. When our English comrades, who had skipped the day's sightseeing, opting for a few hours of relaxation instead, quipped, "Be careful, the water is a bit nippy," I knew I was destined for a very brief, gonad-shrinking dip. Lest we forget, this advice was voiced by a couple who consider a day in the rain, body surfing amongst the rocks on the shore of the North Sea, as the ultimate local recreational activity. The British are not ones for hyperbole, but when my fingers and toes turned the color of the Union Jack, I knew it was time to retreat in favor of a hot shower. The Brits opted for a cold beer, I assume in a frosted glass.

The final group meal of the tour was listed as a farewell "banquet" served, once again, at the hotel's restaurant. The highlight of the evening was the shattering of the seven pointed piñata, which, as we had learned, is the authentic design. No paper mache and crepe paper donkeys, Volkswagens or Green Bay Packers footballs for these intellectuals. Nonetheless, the kids enjoyed scampering for the booty, predominantly hard candies of indeterminate flavors which they took home to New Jersey, undoubtedly to become permanently adhered to the bottom of someone's underwear drawer. Few others in the party were up to the physical manipulations involved with bending over to snag the succulent prizes, lest they return home nursing a slipped disc, dislocated hip or, at the least, pulled hamstring. Being amongst the younger participants of the tour, I should have had the foresight to grab a few sugar bombs myself, in leu of the special farewell "gala" dinner. It consisted of yet another amalgam of cat food and sodden vegetables, this time labeled as "fajitas." Wow, finally, on the final night, a supposedly "authentic" dish native to Mexico. Wrong. As you may have guessed, fajitas actually originated on the cattle ranches of Southern Texas in the early twentieth century. The entrails and undesirable trimmings, such as the diaphragm (or skirt) from slaughtered cows were grilled to feed the Vaqueros (Mexican cowboys) while the American ranch hands, of course, were rewarded with the better cuts. Regardless, better fajitas can be had at most midwestern Irish themed family restaurants. Montezuma subsequently returned for more revenge that evening on select members of our party. Maybe I should have more accurately labeled this final bout of intestinal convulsion as, "Vaqueros' Revenge."

X. FRIDAY, DAY EIGHT: MERIDA TO CANCUN INTERNATIONAL AIRPORT

The bus was set to roll the next morning at 7am. That early departure didn't faze me in the least. I was absorbed by the much anticipated journey back to the familiar icy streets, clean restrooms, personal disrespect and Italian hot dogs of my home state. I set my alarm extra early and tacked on a few additional laps to my morning run around the village square, knowing that we would be constrained in a seated position for the bulk of the day. As I changed into my favorite airplane traveling sweatpants, the ones with the zip off bottoms and multiple velcro pockets, I tuned the TV for a general Northeast US weather report. True to form, CNN was already reporting nine hour delays departing from Newark due to icing conditions. Shocking, freezing weather in February in the New Jersey! A century after the Wright brothers first flights the airlines still haven't managed to anticipate cold weather in winter, heat in the summer and an occasional cloud at any time of year. Arrivals were less severely affected. Unfortunately, our plane spends its day completing a round trip between New Jersey and Cancun. Our beloved early afternoon Continental 737 couldn't land in Mexico if it could not depart from the Garden State. Only the masters of the airline industry could manage to incorporate a nine hour delay into a trip before it had even commenced.

Jeffrey A. Miller

While I am on the subject of transportation mishaps and pitfalls, I would like to provide a word on south of the border rest stops. In a twist of irony to make even Poe envious, the land where E. coli and giarrdhia live freely, unencumbered in performing their beloved task of rampaging the gastrointestinal systems of every foreign tourist in the vicinity, is also home to the most uniformly fetid roadside rest rooms on the continent. The facilities in the museums, archeological sites and hotels are perfectly acceptable, many downright inviting. However, it must be a national joke for the locals to spy the wealthy tourists bounding down the steps of their shining air conditioned vehicles, battling an agonizing war over their digestive tracts against an endless regiment of well armed microbes, forced to seek relief in a squalid nightmare. There are no state-run rest stops, such as commonly found on American highways. Rather, restrooms appear to be managed either in conjunction with a large Pemex service station and adjacent satellite snack and souvenir stand or by free standing, non-franchised restaurants serving empanadas, tacos and ice cream. This would not be such a bad system if the rest stop management was not educated in personal hygiene by an elementary school primer from eleventh century Europe—written in Latin. Fortunately, we have frequented our share of less than impeccable facilities in the US as well, although generally not on the major freeways, so the kids have been well trained in flushing with their feet and touching no exposed surfaces. Sharon, a master of planning the details, always has a supply of alcohol wipes and tissue packets hidden in her backpack.

Toilet paper at these rest stops was the scarcest of commodities, resulting in a cultish following by the women of our tour usually reserved for Bruce Springsteen, the latest version of the ipod, or the newest restaurant from Daniel Baloud. The proprietors used our

Throw Me Under The Bus...Please

bodies' functional needs as one more opportunity to extract a few more pesos from the same back pocket area. You could say their goal was literally to pull money out of one's ass. Even the most revered medieval alchemist would be hard pressed to successfully perform that stunt. There was generally an old man or woman stationed by the entrance to the ladies' room dolling out isolated squares of single ply for five or ten pesos. Extortion at its most basic level. I wouldn't be surprised if the local branch of the Luccesi or Bannono crime families or offshoot of a violent drug smuggling ring didn't have a hand in this affair. Sharon was anointed as champion of the john by the other ladies, however, as she earned renown throughout the group as the woman with the extra roll of toilet paper or packet of tissues always at the ready. Best of all, she handed it out gratis. I begged her to undercut the competition at three pesos per square. Thankfully, she deferred. I would have lived in fear the entire trip that we would wake up one morning with a horse's head buried at the foot of the bed. The take-away message about Mexican rest stops is that even with an adequate supply of imported sanitary products in hand, these stalls are not the preferred environment to sit studying the first section of the international New York Times.

Being an ardent shopper, Raphi, with the support of his equally adept mother, managed to deplete our final pesos at a Pemex station midway to the Cancun International Airport. Sharon found a "Bimbo Bread" bicycle racing shirt to add to her collection. Bimbo, according to Pepe, is the largest baker in the continent and the manufacturer of Wonder Bread in the US. Although she found the double entendre irresistible, I assume the humor goes unnoticed by the majority of the Spanish speaking populace. Raphi made off with an exquisite deep purple velour sombrero, which is now hanging on the wall of his room. Unfortunately, it was about three feet in diameter, tassels, ribbons and all, and would require a fair degree of dexterity and perseverance to maneuver around the cramped bus and plane. Raphi managed the challenge with aplomb and the hat arrived in pristine condition. The same cannot be said for the sunglasses he forgot on the bus, the left sandal missing in action or the note pad ruined by an errant open bottle of water.

As the bus pulled into the airport terminal, we uttered the requisite farewells to Mom and Dad. I hope no one will be surprised if I confess that I am not one for ostentatious or loquacious "goodbyes." I am also not a vociferous donor of "hellos," either. I prefer to drift in and out of locations and situations as an invisible vapor, only acknowledging my presence when I am hungry, tired or most commonly, bored. As for salutations, I take as my mantra the old WC Fields line, "Enough of this lovemaking, let's eat." With a handshake for Dad and a quick peck for Mom, I exited the bus. Sharon and the boys, fortunately, are much more adept in the emotional arts and managed a long rendition of heartfelt hugs, "best wishes" and "thank you's." Tears, however, would have been excessive to the point of sarcasm, and therefore, none were shed. We each grabbed our bags, one wheeled suitcase and one carry-on backpack per traveler. Each was intelligently arranged by Sharon to be of the rolling variety, allowing us to saunter effortlessly towards the check-in desk. Not that we required such efficiency. Even if the plane had been on time, we were still two hours early for the scheduled departure. As is my habit, the moment we stepped through the entrance of the terminal I immediately checked the departing flight monitor.

Our rescue shuttle was officially listed as boarding "on time," which was curious. When I reconnoitered the arrivals monitor, that same plane was shown to have left Newark for the first segment of its round trip journey

Throw Me Under The Bus...Please

three hours late with no touchdown time in Cancun even set. Either the pilots had absconded an F-22 fighter for the trip, which would have left scant room for the 150 odd expectant passengers or Continental Airlines was making a languid attempt to quell a potential passenger revolt. Being a man best served by numbers, I immediately began to calculate best and worst case scenarios of approximately when our flight home would actually commence. Fortunately, if I had acquired nothing else on our sojourn, I learned to accept, and at times, even harness, boredom. A week of sitting on a bus and walking in circles in the parking lots of indistinguishable rest stops in an attempt to avoid blood clots in my legs was making the current situation more tolerable. Compared to the tight confines of the bus, the Airport provided infinitely more room to stroll and a greater variety of sites. I actually relished the notion of creating a personal mini-tour of the myriad of tropical themed bars, chain restaurants and overpriced souvenir stands separating the jet ways. Too bad I couldn't borrow Pepe for a few hours to provide me with the biography of the founder of the "Crab Shack," a precise tally of the combined seating capacity of the waiting areas or dissertation on the intricacies of the bond issue that funded the airport's construction.

    The airport even had one of those uniquely Mexican duty free stores with the tequila tasting station. Sullenly, a shot of purloined booze was infinitely more satisfying as a means of inaugurating our adventure than as a consolation for a day wasted in an overcrowded, whitewashed airline terminal. In fact, Sharon, sulking at the notion of returning to the falling snow and workaday responsibilities of home, deferred a drink. Refusing to be pulled into her funk, I whispered a silent toast to the first person to have devised a means of installing efficient air conditioning on an intercity bus and knocked down a single slug of 12 year-old anejo tequila. Sharon and the boys opted instead to study the display of designer watches adjacent the liquor counter. At times like these, I justify my weakness with the words of one of history's most obstinate, ferocious leaders; none other than Winston Churchill. In my most succinct bastardization of the Queen's English, he is reported to have stated, concerning his favorite vice, "Champagne, in victory I deserve it; in defeat, I need it." Besides, I was already wearing two watches and did not want to be tempted to purchase another.

Of course, the kids know how best to remain entertained when they are bored. They fill their stomachs. Actually, they hadn't eaten all day and were looking forward to something tastier than the usual sterile, outrageously priced airport fair. No such luck. However, in the past week we had evolved not only a tolerance for remaining seated for extended periods of time but also the ability to ignore the protests of our hypersensitive, well educated taste buds. Surprisingly, a skeptical taste of Jared's beef fajita and chili combination platter and equally quizzical sampling of Raphi's chicken fajita with burrito revealed higher quality meats, better seasoned vegetables and riper guacamole than at any of the "gourmet" meals we were promised on the tour. Maybe on our next trip to Mexico, we will stock up on food and free liquor at the airport.

I spent the next three hours pacing up and down the predominantly linear terminal concourse, pausing intermittently to write in my trip diary or accompany Raphi on "shopping trips" to the many identical souvenir shops lining the isles. He kept occupied calculating how much we had saved by purchasing our gifts from the native entrepreneurs at the archeology sites rather than at the airport. We did pretty well. He was especially pleased to discover that a purple felt sombrero similar to, but slightly less ornate than his Pemex rest stop purchase, cost

Throw Me Under The Bus...Please

nearly four times as much at the airport. I constantly checked the departure monitors for any updates on our flight. During the course of my wanderings, I happened upon two pilots wishing to fly as passengers in our plane back to their Newark base. They were rather terse, apparently considering a civilian passenger as myself to be of the enemy camp, attempting to infiltrate their select flyboy fraternity. They did manage, however, with little further explanation, to relate the presence of 18 inches of fresh snow on the ground in Newark. Perfect! Even once the arriving plane landed, we would undoubtedly be stuck on the tarmac for hours in Cancun awaiting clearance to become airborne in the northerly direction.

Already agitated, I of course become increasingly morose. Sharon and the kids have learned from years of experience to keep their distance and basically ignore my existence in these situations. I pace and squirm, mutter invectives at the airline industry and covet thy neighbors who are boarding planes to such civilized wonderlands as Cleveland, Houston and Wichita, which were currently experiencing no such delays. I know, it takes a degree of hubris ("chutzpa" to my Semitic brethren) to fling insults at the returning citizens of those aforementioned tourist hot-spots when one is awaiting a flight to Newark, NJ, of all places. Although there has been much effort recently to rebuild New Jersey's largest city, resulting in pockets of gentrification in the commercial districts, many of the low rise residential neighborhoods haven't stopped burning, literally and figuratively, since the racially divided conflagration of 1968. Nonetheless, I look forward to that final scamper up the jet way into Liberty International's terminal "C" with the zeal of an aging baby boomer awaiting a Led Zeppelin reunion tour.

Finally, at 4:30pm, our plane, which had landed about thirty minutes before, was ready for passengers. We boarded rapidly, three hours late. I am actually gleefully surprised, as I had calculated the total delay as potentially being much longer. Of course, boarding and leaving the tarmac are two entirely different matters. I had filled a small souvenir plastic canteen with the last of a bottle of rather acrid tequila before we left and hid it in my carry on. I figured Sharon and I would need a tipple for the aeronautical cattle drive home. Security was performing random baggage checks as we lined up to board. I loitered near the front of the queue until they began harassing a nattily dressed, approximately 35 year old women traveling with her aged mother and two young children. I surmised the interrogation of such a vicious appearing international criminal would occupy the security agents for a while, and I slipped smoothly onto the plane.

My initial gloating at my suave debauchery was soon quelled, however, as I eyed my assignment. Middle seat, back of the plane. Sharon and the boys occupied a row of their own directly behind me. I scoped the vicinity for crying babies. None, yet. My immediate neighbors soon arrived. A teenaged young man took the window seat. Not perfect, but there were decidedly worse potential seat-mates struggling through the entrance at the front of the plane. Besides, despite my prayers, mute anorexic midgets, the ultimate seatmate, are hard to come by in Cancun these days. The young man's father soon followed. Now I know where all those midgets had gone. The old man must have eaten them. It's one thing for a person to be no stranger to the refrigerator, but does one have to worship its contents as if it were a new bride wearing nothing but a garter and a smile. For some inexplicable reason, the pair declined my seemingly altruistic invitation to switch seats, so they could be positioned side by side. Instead, the father and son spent the bulk of the flight carrying on a conversation about the upcoming high school baseball season, using my centrally located cranium as a microphone. The movie? None. The

Throw Me Under The Bus...Please

flight attendant claimed that the trip was too short. Easy for her to say. She wouldn't have to spend the next three hours unwittingly mediating an ESPN debate, sans celebrity athlete input.

Things were looking up. We parted the gate and were airborne moments after the last passenger had taken her place and snapped her aluminum buckle. Typically, she had spent the previous ten minutes attempting to shoehorn a steamer trunk the size of a phone booth (remember them?) into the overhead bin. Her face turned the color of a maraschino cherry and sinuous arms were transformed into those reminiscent of a Pro Bowl bound outside linebacker as she struggled with the rectangular Frankenstein. Sweat dripped from her chin, and her eyes blared unceasingly at her inanimate foe as if attempting to detect a weakness for an eleventh round knockout punch. Relief came for us all in the form of an equally irate stewardess who slapped a day-glow green sticker on the beast (the suit case not its even more monstrous owner) and dragged it towards the jetway on its way to its new temporary home in the plane's hold.

I awaited the requisite Continental Airlines universal snack with the combination of familiarity and disdain usually reserved for an obnoxious in-law at the Thanksgiving table. With virtually no exception short of a pending Ukrainian nuclear attack or F5 tornado striking their catering headquarters, this consisted of mucinous turkey pastrami on a half frozen roll, three leaves of iceberg lettuce accompanied by a shredded carrot and flaming orange French dressing, a bag of chips and a packaged cookie. I formerly would order the Kosher meal to avoid this fate, but soon learned that airline industry research had somehow concluded that observant Jews ate nothing but brisket, a half-thawed egg chalah roll and a factory sealed serving of cling peaches, even at breakfast. Fortunately, Sharon, ever my watchdog, made sure to

89

purchase a $10 chicken balsamic vinegar salad at the Quick Stop in the terminal. Although far from a gustatory serenade, it would provide a dose of protein and fiber superior in both flavor and nutrition to one of the past week's typical buffet dinners. I poured the last of the tequila from the plastic flask into the ice filled plastic cup reserved, or so the stewardess had thought, for my diet Sprite. Sharon, seated behind me, took hers straight up. My hefty neighbor to the right peaked out of the corner of his eye, straining to ignore my treat. I said nothing and offered no sample. The combination of a petroleum-derived receptacle and recirculated air did little for the flavor of the spirit, anyway.

 I used these final hours of in-flight downtime to ponder my abbreviated attempt at digesting *Pride and Prejudice*. It was obvious my literary charade would be abandoned the moment more pressing matters, such as filling my gas tank, watching Monday Night Football, or reading the comics in the New York Daily News, reemerged in my life. As we have discussed previously, I had begun the book partially in deference to the movie, "Jane Austen's Book Club." In that film, Austen's prose appeared to have a profound, beneficial effect on all those who absorbed them. Furthermore, as Sharon was such a fan, I felt it was a benign means of further connecting with the emotional side of her psyche, aside from our shared admiration for professional boxing and brook trout almondine. Alas, whether or not I had succeeded in my quest to indulge the inner workings of my wife's mind, I could not fathom how anyone, male, female or neuter, could read more than a chapter of Austen's work. Although the book was beautifully constructed in a linguistic sense, both eloquent and refined, the subject matter was absolutely banal. Even if I may have missed some of the social and psychological nuances, I found *Pride and Prejudice* predominantly a study of bored

Throw Me Under The Bus...Please

individuals guarding their emotions behind a maze of humorless propriety necessitated by the morals of the times. The old TV series, "Seinfeld" achieved comedic fortune even though it was famously portrayed as, "being about nothing." Little of substance ever happened to the characters during the humorous machinations of the show. However, although not my favorite television sitcom, it was, at least, usually funny.

Nothing worth reporting ever appeared to occur in *Pride and Prejudice,* either. Alas, it is completely devoid of even the slightest occasion for a chuckle. A true guffaw would require more than just a shot of bourbon and afternoon of tedium but rather something more on the line of a tandem recital of the novel by the ghosts of Henny Youngman and Groucho Marx, in drag. The lack of humor in a book whose major action sequences entail strolling down a country road or dancing a waltz with one's second cousin tends to equate with boredom to my hedonistic tastes. I must admit, though, that I took some delight in the commonality I felt with the book's younger generation as they attempted to borrow the Bennett family horse and buggy. The youths' verbal bartering with their father over the use of the vehicle bore a timeless resemblance to my own teenage pleas for the keys to Dad's Oldsmobile. I am sure the theme will be repeated again, with similar vocabulary and inflection, when Jared and Raphi obtain their driver's licenses. I just may let them use my car if they can ask in prose as fluid and artistic as Ms. Austen's. They will only have to promise not to get any horse deposits on the floor pads or upholstery. I would consider such a quip close enough to a joke to warrant the keys.

We miraculously touched down barely three hours after leaving Cancun and found a gate expeditiously, an uncommon occurrence at Newark. Customs was somehow even more lax in New Jersey than it had been in

Jeffrey A. Miller

Mexico City. Literally, the entire procedure consisted of a weak smile by a bored but friendly uniformed control agent and a prompt stamp on our paperwork. Our bags hit the carousel near the start of the procession and we were in a cab minutes after deplaning. There was no line at the taxi stop, either. Something had to go wrong. Had we mistakenly taken a plane to Omaha, Nebraska, where smiling is actually encouraged, dinner at the Wilobee's is regarded as a major social engagement and traffic is measured in tractors per acre of plowed corn field? The belligerent "conversation" between an incensed Port Authority police officer and an equally insolent limousine driver double-parked to our right thankfully confirmed our return to our beloved hometown. I don't think the term, "schmuck," uttered almost in unison by both the chauffer and the cop, even exists in the Midwest, outside of the Chicago suburbs.

By this time, a freezing rain was coating the newly fallen snow. The streets, however, were well salted and in relatively safe condition. Far fewer than 18 inches of snow, as the pilot had warned, remained on the ground. We zipped home as I, ensconced in the front seat near the driver, gleefully fiddled with the familiar local radio stations. The Knicks were losing to Boston once again, another 12 alarm blaze in Brooklyn left six families homeless and Seventh Avenue would be closed between 42nd and 57th streets until 11pm for the Albanian American Appreciation Day street festival. Ahh, we were home!

One last obstacle remained on the way to our front door. I feared the worst for our driveway. I had little desire to shovel an ice-caked tundra at 9:30 in the evening. But then, another miracle; an act of charity beyond mere dollars, food rations or Girl Scout cookie purchases. Our neighbor had cleared much of our asphalt arctic wasteland with his new 6.5 horsepower, two stage,

Throw Me Under The Bus...Please

Craftsman snow blower, complete with headlight and automatic start. As Sharon would mutter, wistful at the unexpected loss of an opportunity to snicker at her beloved but pigheaded husband slaving in the snow, "Such a guy thing." I am sure Emanuel's benevolence was not a completely altruistic endeavor. What better way could a guy flex his muscles and tout the ferocity of his heavy machinery than to clear a pristine swath of "welcome home" blacktop for an envious neighbor. A man whose garage was lined only with a decrepit arsenal of rusted shovels and bristle-deprived brooms.

The moment we entered the house, after the requisite symphony of fast-paced footsteps and flushing toilets, everyone scattered to his or her private domain, seeking the week's first reintroduction to the concept of personal space. Jared ran to his room to log onto his computer; Raphi hustled to his quarters to re-acquaint himself with his menagerie of stuffed animals; Sharon, in what has become an archaic habit in an age where most of our calls are via cell phone, checked for landline phone messages. Nothing important. She followed up with a shot of bourbon and retired to her favorite chair in our room to finish her book, alone, tuned to a 1940's era cable movie in the background. Always the point-woman on the trip, she relished the opportunity for a few moments of solitude, left to ponder the deluge of laundry that waited the next morning. I, in my designated curse as "father-of-the-bride," even without a daughter or plans for a wedding, was left to "schlep" (sorry, for those of you in the plain states, it is yet another Yiddish term, meaning, "to carry.") the bags and suitcases into the house and down to the laundry area in the basement. I removed all non-washable or non-wearable items from each suitcase. The remaining flotsam of soiled clothing would be Sharon's burden now. I logged into each of my work-related computers to make sure no major system failures had occurred in my absence. Fortunately, none had. A reliable power supply is one of the advantages of living in the shadows of the local high tension wires. The disadvantage, of course, besides acting as a convenient conduit for herds of deer to gain easy access to our yard, is the deleterious effects the towers have on the resale value of one's house.

Our previous home was also adjacent high tension line stanchions. I remember standing by our realtor as, one after another, potential purchasers would ply their 350 pound frames from their unbuckled car seats. They were invariable chain smoking as they waddled up the driveway, still chewing the remnants of the fourth jelly donut of the morning. Their initial smiles at the near pristine condition of our house soon reverted to sneers as they spied the power lines along the side of the yard, muttering something to the effect of, "Those high-tension lines are a killer! All that EMF can cause brain cancer, ya know." I still am not sure why such morons would worry about the health of the only bodily organ they did not appear to possess.

I checked my email and found the usual array of unfiltered "spam" and updates from various radiology professional sites. I ran outside to collect the day's newspapers, half buried in the snow at the foot of the driveway. I grabbed a diet orange Sunkist soda from the fridge, poured it over crushed ice for good measure, scooped a spoon full of chocolate ice-cream from the freezer and walked back up to my office to read the headlines before retiring.

As I headed back down to bed, I remembered our Italian food takeout order, placed before we left. I grudgingly opened the front door, reeling initially from the hereto unnoticed wind. The house was so cold, however, as we had turned down the heat during our absence, that I noticed little change in temperature as I

Throw Me Under The Bus...Please

leaned outdoors. No bag or box was identified. Only a small amount of snow had blown onto the porch, but I could not see any unusual four-legged footprints or hoof prints, either. No red or green food remnants were identified. My years in New Jersey have left me somewhat of an expert in the destructive habits of the native fauna. Rabbits and ground hogs have little interest in tomato sauce and mozzarella cheese, and were unlikely candidates for thievery. They prefer to reap havoc by digging boroughs in the most tenuous of structural weight bearing turf, such as beneath the house or under the aeration waterfalls in our gold fish pond. I am sure the foundation of our house is teetering on collapse, as most of the surrounding soil has been removed to provide a network of underground boroughs. There must be at least one enterprising ground hog who has published a guide in the manner of a New York City subway map just to aid in the navigational of that underground metropolis. Some mornings I could swear I see them, miniature cups of coffee and tiny newspapers in hand, streaming from the distant corners of the yard towards the teaming subterranean assemblage beneath our house. Hawks and falcons could have theoretically swooped down and grabbed our Italian feast, but they tend to stay far away from homes and cement. They prefer moving targets. Deer, although theoretically vegetarians, seem to derive satisfaction from using their considerable bulk to trample, dislodge and otherwise annihilate anything they happen to encounter, even if not within their normal narrow dietary range. I could perceive no such haphazard damage in the area. The most likely culprit in this apparent caloric thievery, therefore, appeared to be a raccoon. They are both intelligent and diligent and are adept at obtaining almost anything they set their devious minds upon. Furthermore, as active scavengers, they are happy to dine on virtually anything and make little distinction between

Italian food, Chinese fare, week old garbage or a misplaced mitten. They are not alone. I have been to many restaurants in my life that also refrain from such culinary distinctions. However, as bright as they are, raccoons do not have the patience to sweep their paths behind them, and almost always leave a trail of little, almost humanoid footprints in their wake. In the end, I surmised that the pizzeria forgot to deliver our order in the first place. Even more likely, the pizzeria still intended to send our meal. They were either just "too busy" to compile our request in less than a week or they had a new delivery boy, not well versed in the local environs, who was still driving in endless circles, praying that by some coincidence he would eventually arrive at our front door before he received his first social security check. If he ever arrives, I promise to still tip him a couple bucks for his troubles.

POSTSCRIPT

I must relate one final bit of irony in a sojourn crammed with a myriad of similar diabolical twists of fate. As we scuttled down the narrow stairs of the bus for the final time at the Cancun International Airport, Mom and Dad headed off for two days of glorious, educationally vapid relaxation at that city's renowned bleached white beaches. Due to work-related obligations and the difficulty in arranging flights for four individuals during the traditional Presidents' Week mayhem, we were unable to join them in their aquatic paradise. The eldest generation of the Miller clan, who had nothing but disdain for the traditional vacation-inspired "vices" of pleasure and decompression, were free to frolic in the surf. Not a museum, ancient artifact or buffet table in site. Their offspring, who desired nothing from their holiday but warm breezes, cool water and cold beer, were subjugated to a week of service in a paramilitary regiment of amateur archeologists, with nary a moment free to enjoy such pursuits.

Paradoxically, as punishment for my parent's hypocrisy, the Almighty invoked the "Law of Just Deserts," which is basically a slightly crueler corollary of "Murphy's Law." We learned that when Mom and Dad arrived at their four star hotel, sans bugs and wake up calls, of course, they were informed that their room was not yet ready. Evidently, Pepe and his corporate-backed wheel-greasing, which had induced such an effortless transition between destinations during the tour, were no longer an influence. Rather than lounge at the beach with their bags and street clothes (I don't recall which of his two t-shirts Dad was wearing at the time), they opted for lunch at a recommended establishment. Although quite near their resort, a week of being herded about like a pair of lobotomized termites had dampened their usually sharp senses of direction. By the time they found the desired restaurant, it was approaching mid afternoon. Lunch, itself, was fraught with its own set of service delays and culinary bungles. Needless to say, by the time they arrived back at the hotel, it was already getting dark. Nearly an entire day in the tropics completely wasted.

If this was a work of fiction, I might have reported that Mom and Dad were unable to procure a cab after their meal and were forced to take a bus back to their hotel. However, that would be almost too stilted a manipulation of the plot, made obvious by its shear improbability. In truth, the restaurant manager called for a taxi, which served as the sole positive highlight of their day. Having served their afternoon of penitence, the final day in Cancun was quite enjoyable and flight home relatively uneventful.

The following day, as I unpacked, I reflected upon what revelations the trip had provided about the members of the Miller family and their interpersonal relations. In short, not many. I am still impressed by my parents' intellect and energy and disparaged by their egos. Sharon remains my best friend, object of my romantic desires, and my primary support. Jared and Raphi continue to both embellish me with pride and sadden me with nostalgia as I observe their evolution from adorable children into fascinating, complex, mature human beings. We all gained an appreciation of the sophistication of pre-Columbian Meso-American culture and all, except I am sure, Dad, forgot virtually every fact and anecdote we had

Throw Me Under The Bus...Please

learned on our journey. I felt as if I had just finished finals week in college. The only instructional details I remembered were the ones that were already firmly entrenched in my grey matter prior to our sojourn. Most of the knowledge crammed into our brains in the past week was lost the moment we opened the front door, sucked by the vacuum of the hallway into the heating ducts, destined for incineration in the basement furnace.

In short, our expedition to the monotonous highways and overtly reconstructed archeological sites had changed nothing of the inner fabric of our family or our minds. However, we now have some attractive ceramic dishes and bowls, broken onyx statuettes, a burnt parchment rendition of an emperor-astronaut, and an ornate purple sombrero to adorn our abodes. We have even assembled a purposely mismatched set of Tala Vera earthenware, ordered from the internet, of course, to use as our everyday dinner set. As you can see, in the spirit of true capitalism, the only tangible remnants of our short educational campaign are material goods, easily replaceable with the click of a mouse or short ride to the mall. With that in mind, next year we will just go to Miami, San Juan, or the Bahamas and spend the week aimlessly frolicking in the surf and eating fresh fish of an identified species ordered from a real menu. I will leave the Austen novels at the bookstore but promise to page through a few back editions of *National Geographic* in leu of a guided bus ride between fields of reconstructed stone temples.

www.ingramcontent.com/pod-product-compliance
Lightning Source LLC
Chambersburg PA
CBHW031653040426
42453CB00006B/286